Financial Risk Analysis

An AMA Management Briefing

L. Daniel Maxim
Frank X. Cook, Jr.

 American Management Association, Inc.

658.15
M464

© American Management Association, Inc., 1972.
All rights reserved. Printed in the United States of America.

This Management Briefing has been distributed to all members enrolled in the Finance Division of the American Management Association. A limited supply of extra copies is available at $5.00 a copy for AMA members, $7.50 for nonmembers.

This publication may not be reproduced, stored in a retrieval system, or transmitted in whole or in part, in any form or by any means, electronic, mechanical, photocopying, recording, or otherwise, without the prior written permission of the Association.

International standard book number: 0-8144-2153-9
Library of Congress catalog card number: 72-182226

First printing

Financial Risk Analysis

L. Daniel Maxim is Director of Operations Research for MATHEMATICA, a research and consulting firm in Princeton, New Jersey. He is also Adjunct Professor of Industrial Engineering at Newark College of Engineering. Before joining MATHEMATICA, Mr. Maxim was employed by National Starch and Chemical Corporation, where he directed a group conducting research in physical chemistry, applied statistics, process optimization, and operations research. He has published numerous articles in professional journals and is a frequent contributor to American Management Association seminars. He holds degrees from Manhattan College, Syracuse University, and Stevens Institute of Technology, and is currently a doctoral candidate in operations research at New York University.

Frank X. Cook, Jr. is a staff consultant with MATHEMATICA, where his research and consulting interests include risk analysis, corporate planning models, production models, and military systems analysis. Before joining MATHEMATICA, Mr. Cook was a design engineer and systems analyst with Grumman Aerospace Corporation. A mechanical engineer by training, Mr. Cook holds degrees from Manhattan College, City College of New York, and Stevens Institute of Technology. He is also a frequent contributor to American Management Association seminars.

The hallmark of the great generals, the Wellingtons and Marlboroughs and Nelsons, has been their extreme skill in working out the risk.

Antony Jay
Management and Machiavelli

Preface

Few would argue that the presence of uncertainty is the key element that serves to distinguish between routine action and tough decision. The successful decision maker is one who has a high tolerance for uncertainty and ambiguity, the ability to assess the likelihood and impact of uncertain events on decision options, and, finally, the courage to make decisions in the face of imperfect information. This briefing addresses the second of these attributes, the ability to calculate the odds and weigh the risks of alternative courses of action.

In the past, "calculations" of odds have been highly unstructured and implicit. More recently, there have been developed a series of mathematical tools and techniques that can materially contribute to explicit consideration of risk and uncertainty.* Collectively, the new techniques are known as risk analysis. In the relatively short time since its inception, risk analysis has proved useful in both government and industry. We have had the fortunate experience of participating in a large number of risk analyses in each area.

The specific focus of this briefing is on the use of risk analysis in capital-budgeting problems. As we will discuss in Chapter 1, decisions on capital investment are among the toughest and most important ones with which top management is faced. It is the experience of many firms that an analytical methodology, if well structured, disciplined, and well executed, pays handsome dividends in improved decision making in the vital capital investment area. We have attempted to convey the spirit, concept, and techniques of that methodology in this briefing. Basically the methodology is a synthesis of modern economic and accounting concepts and the tools and techniques of operations research and management science imbedded in the framework of systems analysis.

We hope that this briefing will be useful to both executives and managers who wish an overview and appreciation of risk analysis and to practicing analysts who seek to gain further insight into their craft. For that reason we have refrained from making the briefing highly technical; instead, we provide a large number of references that elaborate on the technical aspects of risk analysis. For the benefit of readers who are generally unfamiliar with the areas of probability, statistics, and mathematical models, we have included a chapter that introduces those concepts. We have also included a chapter that reviews current criteria for selection of investments, because those concepts may be unfamiliar to some readers (witness the success of American Management Association seminars that address that subject).

---

*Economists and decision theorists generally distinguish between risk and uncertainty. The distinction is indeed useful in certain contexts, but it will not be made here and we will use the terms interchangeably.

We would like to acknowledge the helpful discussions with our colleagues at MATHEMATICA, particularly those with Oskar Morgenstern, Norman Agin, Robert Christie, Stephen Robinson, and Gene Prescott. Much gratitude is due also to Mrs. Patricia Klensch for fine typing of the manuscript and Thomas Gannon of the American Management Association for inviting us to write this briefing and his encouragement throughout our effort. Finally, we are grateful to the editors at Addison-Wesley, Doubleday, *Harvard Business Review*, and The Rand Corporation for their kind permission to publish selected quotations. Of course, the responsibility for errors and omissions rests solely with the authors.

L. Daniel Maxim
Frank X. Cook, Jr.

Contents

1 Introduction and Overview / 1

2 Selection of Investment Criteria / 11

3 Mathematical Tools for Risk Analysis / 21

4 Obtaining Inputs to a Risk Analysis / 33

5 Interrelated Decisions Over Time / 41

6 Intellectual Post-Processing / 49

References / 59

The only sure thing in this world is the past, but all we have to work with is the future.

August Detoeuf
Comments of a Candy-Maker

1
Introduction and Overview

Decisions regarding capital and associated expenditures are among the toughest and most important of those facing top management. They are important for several reasons. First, they usually involve the commitment of substantial amounts of money.[1] Second, they involve a commitment to action over an extended time frame and thus consume other valuable corporate resources (for example, time of executive and technical personnel, which might be otherwise allocated). Third, the decisions have a high visibility, or what one writer terms a "bricks-and-mortar permanence" (recall Du Pont's Corfam, Ford's Edsel, General Dynamics' TFX, and Boeing's SST) that serves as a constant reminder of poor past decisions.

Capital decisions are tough because uncertainty masks the optimal course of action. In many industries, the fraction of new products that are successful is no higher than 0.1 to 0.3; yet 30 to 40 percent of profits may be derived from products launched within the preceding 5 years. Uncertainty may fairly be said to be the dominant characteristic of capital investment decisions. Pierre Massé (16) provides a quote from Keynes that reflects the expressed attitude of many businessmen.

> The crucial point in this field is the extremely fragile nature of the data upon which we must perforce make our estimates of discounted returns. Our knowledge of the factors that govern the yield on an investment a few years hence is generally very limited, and sometimes negligible. Frankly, we must admit that in order to estimate the profits on a railroad ten years, or even five years, hence, or those of a copper mine, a textile mill, a brand of drugs, a transatlantic steamer or a building in London, the available data really boil down to very little, and sometimes to absolutely nothing.

Conventional Investment Analysis

In sharp contrast with the acknowledged uncertainty of capital investment decisions, conventional analysis procedures are almost deterministic in concept and execution. The typical investment analysis procedure requires the specification of most likely (or in some cases the expected) value of each of the factors that enter into the calculation of investment return. By use of those values (for example, net present worth, payback period, return

---

[1] For the past few years, total private domestic investment (which includes both costs of structures and producer's durable equipment) has been hovering about the $100 billion mark annually. (21) That is roughly 20 percent of the value of goods sold and 10 percent of total final sales of goods and services. Impressive as the figure is, it understates the total costs associated with capital expenditures because many associated costs, for example, advertising costs, are expensed rather than capitalized. The other costs are often of magnitude comparable with that of the largest capital expenditures.

on investment) the worth of the investment is determined, and the result is presented to management. To be sure, everyone concerned realizes that uncertainty surrounds the number, but under the conventional procedure the uncertainty is not made explicit. The evaluation of the likelihood and consequence of investment return that differs from the calculated value is left as an implicit process. (The implicit process has a certain mystique often described in reverential terms such as "judgment and wisdom."

Conventional analysis procedures may not only fail to consider uncertainty explicitly (and so fail to produce any estimate of the range and likelihood of possible outcomes) but also even fail to produce the correct average or expected investment return in the presence of uncertainty. We will illustrate that statement with an example. Suppose we are conducting an investment analysis on a proposed chemical plant of 5 million pounds annual capacity. Demand for the product is estimated to average 5 million pounds in the third year of operation. In a deterministic analysis we would estimate sales to be the smaller of plant capacity or demand, in this case 5 million pounds. In fact, however, there is often considerable uncertainty in demand estimates—and possibly some uncertainty in the estimate of capacity, as well, but that is typically a second-order effect.

Let's see what impact that uncertainty in demand is likely to have on our expected sales. Suppose we had asked our marketing experts to give us information on the relative likelihood that the product demand would be any of several values, say, from 3 to 7 million pounds in the third year. (Chapter 4 tells you how to elicit that information in a systematic way.) Their response might be as shown in Figure 1-1. Now let us reexamine the problem of estimating sales. Since our plant capacity is 5 million pounds, it is impossible for sales to be any greater than 5 million pounds; but inspection of Figure 1-1 shows that it is certainly possible for demand (and hence sales) to fall *below* 5 million pounds. Thus it is impossible for *average* sales to be equal to 5 million pounds. In fact, the actual average value of sales in this case is 4.8 million pounds, as computed in the technical footnote.[2] The important point is not the details of computation, but the fact that a deterministic analysis gave us a *biased* result when uncertainty was present. Moreover, the amount of the bias is directly proportional to the magnitude of this uncertainty.

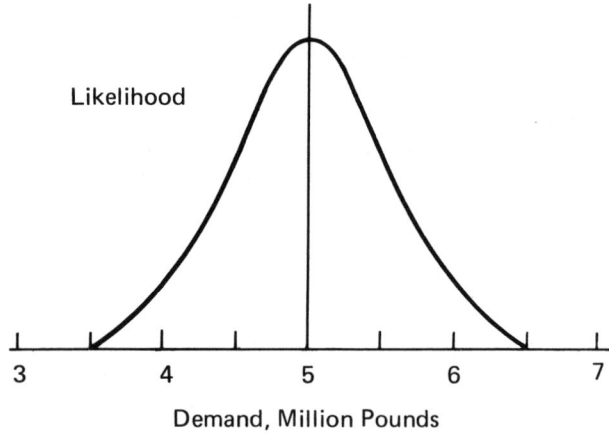

Figure 1-1. Likelihood profile for product demand.

Thus there are two important limitations to conventional analysis in the presence of uncertainty:

1. The procedures do not give information on the range and likelihood of possible investment outcomes.
2. The procedures may not even give the expected investment outcome accurately.

Improvements to Conventional Parameters

Faced with the shortcomings of conventional procedures, businessmen and analysts have sought alternatives. Hertz (11), among others, has listed some of those alternative approaches, which are shown in the box below. They are useful to varying degrees, but all are limited.

Previous Approaches to Handling Uncertainty in Capital Investment Decisions

1. Use of criteria that emphasize liquidity.
2. Development of more accurate forecasts.
3. Subjective post-processing and implicit risk discounting.
4. Comparison with previous projects and empirical adjustments of expectation.
5. Worst case–best case analysis.

Useful But Limited

---

[2] Let x be the annual demand and c the plant capacity. Then the actual sales s is given by the following equations:

$$s = x \quad \text{if} \quad x \leq c$$
$$s = c \quad \text{if} \quad x > c$$

If f_x and F_x respectively denote the density function and cumulative distribution function of the random variable x, the expected level of sales $E[s]$ is given by

$$E[s] = F_x(c) \int_0^c x f_x(x)\, dx + [1 - F_x(c)]\, c$$

Brown (3) gives convenient tables for solution of the preceding equation for the case when x is normally distributed and, in particular, for the case when $\mu = 5$, $\sigma = 0.5$, then $E[s] = 4.8$.

The first (and in our view, the worst) of the other approaches is to use as criteria for evaluating investment worth those that emphasize liquidity. (An example is the use of payback as a composite measure of risk and return. As we shall see in detail in Chapter 2, payback is a measure of neither risk nor return.) With reference to the two limitations of conventional analysis cited earlier, it is clear that the mere substitution of one criterion of investment worth for another does not provide us with information on the range or likelihood of possible investment outcomes or necessarily reduce the bias in the estimation of expected investment worth.

Another approach is to reduce the uncertainty in investment outcome by increasing the accuracy of estimation of the input factors. An example of the approach is the test marketing of a new product to obtain an estimate of demand, price, and effects of advertising levels prior to wider distribution. In essence this approach amounts to buying information on which a decision to commit substantial resources can be based. There are many circumstances in which the practice is both feasible and desirable, but even then the uncertainty is at best reduced and not eliminated: the problem of estimating uncertainty remains. Also, there are circumstances in which the purchase of information is impossible or impractical.

Still another approach is to have managers and executives estimate the aggregate uncertainty of investment outcome. Here wisdom and judgment come into play. Proposed investments are classified as high risk, moderate risk, or riskless, and, typically, a different standard of profitability is then applied to each category. For example, high-risk investments might be expected to earn at least 18 percent after taxes, whereas riskless investments might be required to earn only 12 percent. We find no fault with the notion of a risk-based investment acceptance criterion. The limitation of the approach is simply the difficulty associated with making accurate judgments of aggregate investment risk on a subjective basis. Moreover, it is impossible to form accurate perceptions of the bias in the expected investment outcome.

A variant of the subjective approach is to make empirical adjustments to the calculated measure of investment worth based upon previous corporate experience with similar calculations. For example, a study of cost overruns on major weapon systems in the fifties and early sixties, conducted by Peck and Scherer, indicated that the average ratio of actual cost to anticipated cost was about 3.2 and ranged from less than 1 to about 7. Thus, when the Department of Defense estimated the cost of the ABM system at $7 billion, the *New York Times* estimated over $20 billion. The validity of the approach hinges on the assumption that the future will behave like the past (no learning on our part, constant economic conditions, and so on). In his famous parable *Leopards in the Temple* Franz Kafka (14) illustrates how such extrapolation can become absurd:

> Leopards break into the temple and drink to the dregs what is in the sacrificial pitchers; this is repeated over and over again; finally it can be calculated in advance, and it becomes a part of the ceremony.

Quite apart from that consideration, it is necessary, in order to employ the adjustment technique with any degree of precision, to have a substantial data base from which to make projections. It is unlikely that such a data base is available to many firms, and so the technique is of limited utility.

The fifth approach is what has been termed worst case-best case analysis. Managers are asked to provide three estimates of each of the investment factors: a pessimistic value, or worst case, that is almost certain to be exceeded, a most likely value, and an optimistic value, or best case. The optimistic and pessimistic values of each investment factor are then combined to give optimistic and pessimistic values of the investment outcome. Table 1-1 provides a simple illustration of the procedure. In the example, the combination of all worst-case values yields a net present worth (NPW) of -$81, whereas the combination of optimistic values yields an NPW of $55.

The worst case-best case has two basic advantages. First, it provides useful information if the data are gathered with care; second, it is easy to apply and understand. On the other hand, although it provides information on the range of possible values, no estimate of the *likelihood* of those (or other) values can be obtained. Two investments can have the same range of outcomes but have widely differing risks. Thus, at best, the worst case-best case approach provides only a partial answer to the problem of assessing risk in capital investment. A second disadvantage is that different individuals have quite different notions of the probabilities associated with the words "optimistic" and "pessimistic." The point is made nicely by Donald H. Woods (23) in the *Harvard Business Review:*

> These supposedly widely understood terms open up the possibility of very different interpretations and to some extent may even encourage political manipulation because of their ambiguity. For example, the range from the optimistic to the pessimistic level could vary widely between two information specialists, even though they both guess the actual uncertainty to be about the same. Far from helping to resolve uncertainty, therefore, these ambiguous everyday procedures may even increase it.

In order to use the approach for comparison of alternative investments, it is essential that all experts who furnish information employ the same working definitions for the terms.

Table 1-1. Illustration of worst case-best case analysis.

	Year 0
Low	150
High	200

(a) Investment Outlays

	Year			
	0	1	2	3
Low		40	50	70
High		60	80	140

(b) Cash Returns

		Worst Case		Best Case	
Year	Flow	Discount Factor at 15%	Discounted Flow	Flow	Discounted Flow
0	-200	1.000	-200.00	-150	-150.00
1	40	0.869	34.75	60	52.14
2	50	0.756	37.80	80	60.48
3	70	0.658	46.06	140	92.12
Net present worth*			- 81.39		54.74

*But what is the *relative likelihood* of these values?

(c) Determination of Range of Net Present Worth

New Approaches to Risk Analysis

The limitations of the previous approaches to handling uncertainty in capital investment analysis, coupled with the importance of the decisions concerned, have provided the impetus for the development of techniques that permit explicit consideration of uncertainty. Although the techniques differ somewhat (for example, analytical versus simulation methods), they are identical in concept and follow basically the same sequence of operations. (See Refs. 1, 2, 5-7, 9, 10, 12, 13, 15, 17-19, and 22.) First, a set of relations between relevant investment factors and investment outcomes is specified.

The relations, known as models, permit calculation of measures of investment worth from values of the investment factors. This first step is identical with the first step of conventional analysis.

The second step involves the determination of a *probability distribution* for each of the variables identified in the first step. For example, suppose that one of the variables of interest is the project life in years. A distribution for that variable, Figure 1-2(a), specifies the probability that the project will last 1 year, 2 years, . . . , n years. We see that the project is estimated to have a 20 percent chance of terminating in 3 years, a 40 percent chance of terminating in 4 years, a 20 percent chance of terminating in 5 years, and so on.

Figure 1-2. Inputs to a risk analysis.

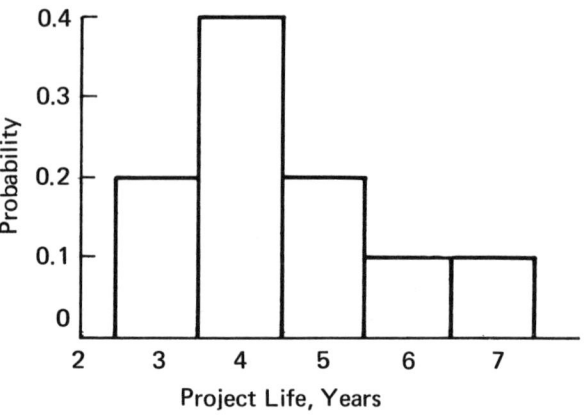

(a) Probability Mass Function

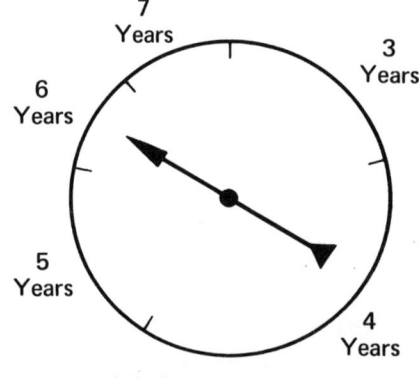

(b) Simulation Device

(Otherwise called a spinner)

The third step is to combine the probability distributions for the input factors to determine a probability distribution for the measure(s) of investment worth. There are basically two kinds of methods that can be employed: the analytical or quasi-analytical methods (Refs. 1, 5, 15, 19, 22) and the simulation methods (Refs. 2, 6, 7, 9, 11, 13, 15). Each kind has advantages and disadvantages. In our view, simulation methods have a slight edge over analytical methods because of their flexibility and, particularly, the ease with which they can be understood. We will therefore focus on simulation throughout this book (see Chapter 3).

The basic notion of the simulation method is to draw random samples from the specified probability distributions for the investment variables and by using those samples, determine a measure of investment worth. The sequence of actions is termed a simulation trial. The process is repeated a large number of times, say, 200 to 1,000. The results of the simulation trials can be assembled to give a likelihood profile for the investment as a whole.

Figure 1-2(b) shows a simple device for sampling from a probability distribution. The lengths of the arcs corresponding to the sectors are directly proportional to the probability of occurrence of the project life. For example, the arc length corresponding to the 3-year sector on the spinner is 20 percent of the circumference of the spinner. If the arrow is equally likely to come to rest at any point on the circumference of the circle, there is a 20 percent chance that the arrow will point to the 3-year sector. To conduct a simulation trial we spin the arrow and record the point at which it comes to rest (6 years is shown). That determines the value of the project life to be used for the trial. Similarly, we exercise other spinners that are built to represent the other investment variables. Figure 1-3, taken from Ref. 2, illustrates the simulation process schematically. The spinner is, of course, just a pedagogical device to illustrate the concept of simulation. In actual practice, computer random number generation schemes are employed.

Illustration of Risk Analysis

NCS Chemical Company is considering the introduction of a new chemical designed to increase the efficiency of production of coated paper. The product has certain unique characteristics, and initial trials by paper mills have yielded impressive results. Future demand for the product is uncertain, however, owing to the characteristics of the marketplace (competition), the fact that the product has a fairly high unit price, and, finally, some uncertainty over the performance of the product under different paper-processing conditions. To compound matters, existing manufacturing facilities cannot be used for the product, and thus a capital investment is required.

Initial analysis of the problem has indicated that there are 19 variables about which some uncertainty exists. For example, the plant investment required is estimated to be $2.2 million, but values from $2.0 to $2.6 million are thought possible. Similar statements can be made for various fixed and variable costs, sales, price, and attrition and growth rates for the variables over time.

Figure 1-3. Overview of the simulation process. (Adapted from Ref. 2.)

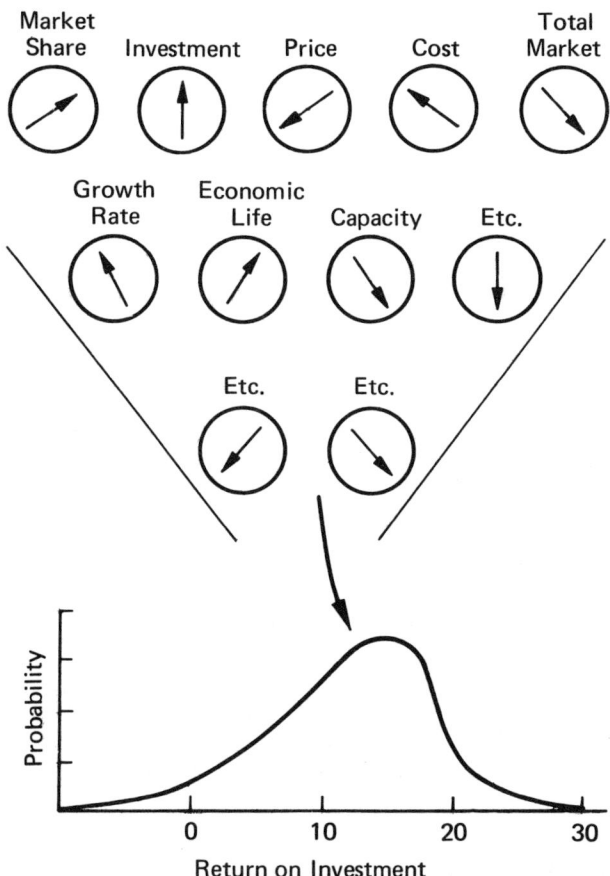

Table 1-2 specifies the uncertainty in costs, price, and demand. In all cases the likelihood profiles for the inputs are triangular in shape. An example of such a profile for demand in year 1 is shown in Figure 1-4. Triangular distributions are quite versatile and can be used to represent a variety of uncertainty profiles, either symmetrical or skewed right or left. For that reason they are frequently employed in risk analysis. However, many alternative distributions are used. We chose triangular profiles for simplicity in this illustration.

Table 1-2. Inputs to example risk analysis. (All values in thousands of dollars unless otherwise specified.)

Scenario: surprise-free. **Alternative:** large plant.

Investment Variables

Cost: Optimistic = 2000; most likely = 2,200; pessimistic = 2,600
Year: Year 0
Capacity: 5,000 units
Depreciation scheme: Sum of years digits 20-year lifetime for tax purposes, straight line for balance sheet purposes

Cost and Revenue

Description*	Initial Value			Growth Rate (% year)		
	Optimistic	Likely	Pessimistic	Optimistic	Likely	Pessimistic
1. Fixed cost 1	250	290	340	2	3	4
2. Fixed cost 2	70	90	110	2	3	4
3. Variable costs ($/unit)						
Raw material	0.24	0.26	0.28	-2	0	1
Processing	0.07	0.08	0.09	-1	0	1
Distribution	0.04	0.06	0.07	-1	0	2
4. Price ($/unit)	0.85	0.85	0.85	-7	-4	-2
5. Demand (000 units)						
Year 1	700	1,000	1,400	NA	NA	NA
2	2,300	3,000	3,500			
3	3,100	4,000	5,000			
4	3,500	4,500	6,000			
5	4,000	5,000	7,000			
6	4,000	5,000	7,000			

*Input distributions assumed triangular.

Figure 1-4. Profile for demand in year 1.

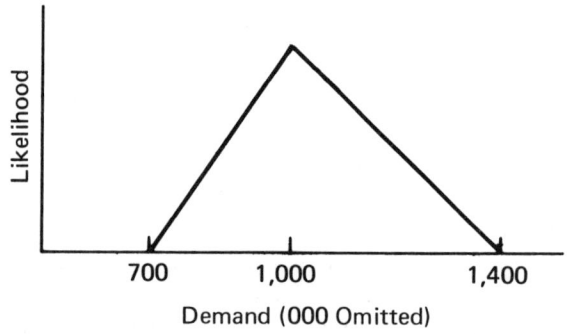

Figure 1-5 shows a schematic model used to calculate cash flows for the NCS venture analysis.[3] NCS management uses net present worth at a discount rate of 16 percent as an investment yardstick. That choice of discount rate resulted not from cost-of-capital considerations (which might be perhaps 10 percent for most companies), but instead from the company's past earnings record. Positive NPW's therefore represent the value of an investment over and above that required to sustain corporate earnings at historical levels. Negative values do not necessarily represent losses in an absolute sense, but are instead to be interpreted as capital return "shortfalls" from desired earnings.

[3] For illustrative purposes a simplified model of the investment was chosen:
(1) Autocorrelation of demand data has been neglected.
(2) Demand-price relationships have been specified as marginal distributions only.
(3) Residual or salvage value of the investment has been assumed zero.
(4) No explicit policies for terminating unsuccessful investments (cutting your losses) have been incorporated.
(5) No explicit capacity expansion policies in the presence of high annual demands have been incorporated.

An actual analysis would incorporate some or all of these options explicitly.

Figure 1-5. Cash flow model for year t.

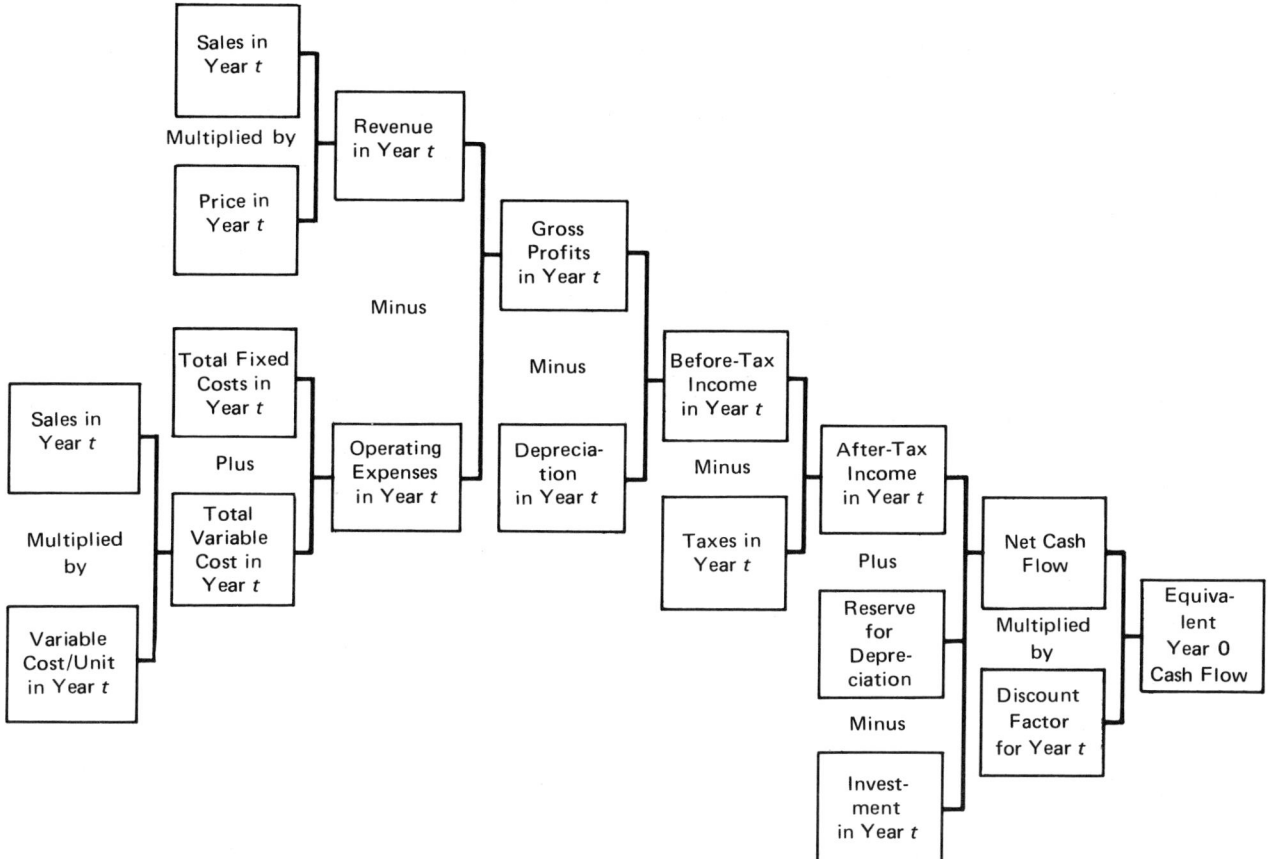

Figure 1-6 shows a facsimile of a computer output that describes results of 200 trials of the investment simulation based upon the input factors listed in Table 1-2. The numbers to the right of the histogram bars are the fractions of trials that resulted in NPW's in the intervals shown on the vertical axis. For example, in about 7 percent of the cases (14 trials) NPW's between 142,500 and 183,500 resulted. Inspection of the histogram shows that there is about a 50 percent chance that the proposed venture will have a positive NPW, that is, about an even money bet that the investment will produce a return equal to or greater than the company's long-term average. The average value of NPW is slightly negative (about $9,000). Should the investment "lose" money, the average loss is about $185,000. On the other hand, there is about a 20 percent chance of the NPW being higher than $200,000.

Note how inspection of the distribution of possible investment returns enables NCS executives to have a clear picture of the uncertainty surrounding the investment alternative. They have not only an unbiased estimate of the average investment worth but also information on the likelihood of obtaining other investment outcomes. NCS's analysis is far from finished at this point (see Chapters 5 and 6 for details on where to go from here), but even this first cut has provided important information.

What Risk? (A Slight Digression)

The problems facing NCS management have to do with what might be termed the *profitability risk* of the venture; that is, NCS is concerned with the risk that the proposed venture will not have acceptable profitability. There are other possible risks. Perhaps the most common one is what might be termed a *liquidity risk*, that is, a risk that the project might require more liquid assets than NCS can furnish, even though it has acceptable profitability. If the project is not of sufficient magnitude to create an unpleasant cash position, it is still possible that the total cash drain of the project, together with the balance of the project "portfolio," will be of sufficient magnitude to cause concern. Thus, management may be concerned with the likelihood of various cash flows *in each time period* as well as the aggregate investment return.

Figure 1-6. Results of simulation runs for example problem.

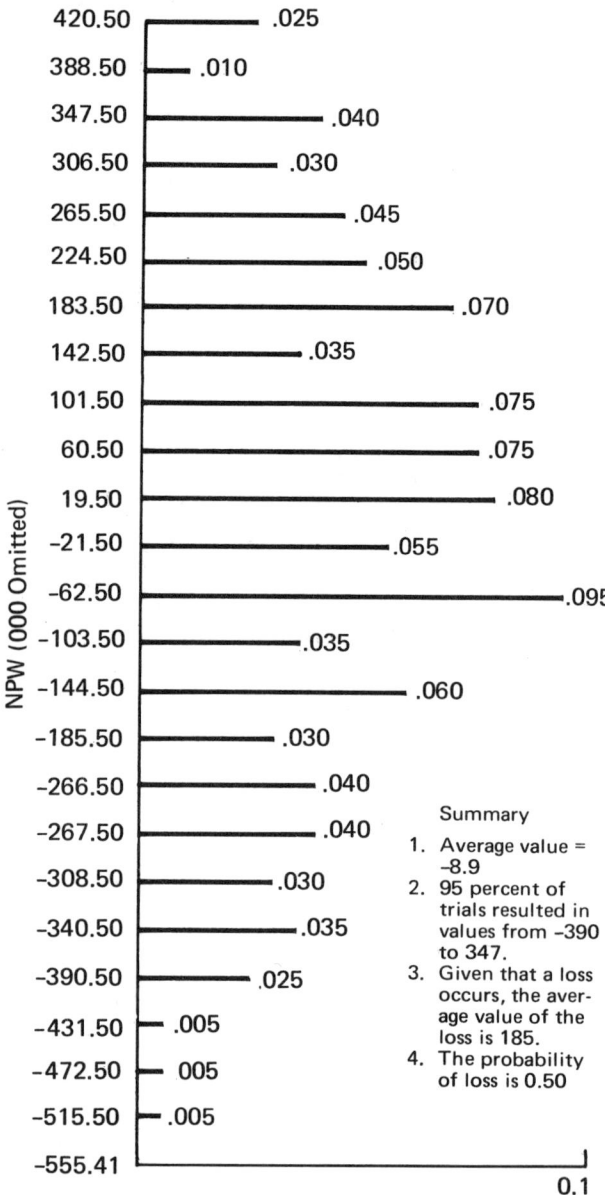

The techniques of risk analysis that were employed to give the distribution of net present worth can be employed to generate the distribution of cash flows for the project (or the entire set of accepted projects) for each time period. Several examples of that use of risk analysis technique are furnished by Mao (15), who also discusses how the information can be used in evaluating alternative venture financing schemes and in cash management generally.

Perspectives on the Risk Analysis Process

The preceding example illustrates the overall concepts and techniques of risk analysis. The basic operational concept is what might be termed a decomposition principle: that of breaking down the problem into smaller elements about which more is likely to be known. For example, the answer to the question what is the probability that the sales price of a product will exceed $x is likely to be known with more precision than the answer to the question what is the probability that NPW of an investment will exceed $y. That is true because, in order to answer the second question, you must *simultaneously* consider the uncertainties of a great many more factors and *how those uncertainties combine* to produce uncertainty in NPW. The first question requires consideration of only one factor. It may be difficult to evaluate the likelihood profile for a given factor, but it is in precisely those circumstances that the risk analysis approach is most useful. David Hertz (11) makes this point forcefully and cogently when he states:

> It cannot be emphasized too strongly that the less certainty there is in an "average" estimate, the more important it is to consider the possible variation in that estimate.
>
> Further, an estimate of the variation possible in a factor, no matter how judgmental it may be, is always better than a simple "average" estimate, since it includes more information about what is known and what is not known. It is, in fact, this very lack of knowledge which may distinguish one investment possibility from another, so that for rational decision making it must be taken into account.

Not all executives would agree with that statement, however. The following remark made by Harlan Meal, quoted in Brown (4), illustrates a typical attitude:

> When the information quality is so poor that the assignment of probabilities to outcomes seems an exercise in futility, decision theory analysis can be most useful. Yet most executives in such a situation say that the only thing which really can be useful is their own experienced intuition. The executive is going to behave as though he has information about the situation, whether he has it or not.

In order to make effective use of risk analysis, managers and executives have to learn to think probabilistically. For many, that comes quite naturally, but for others a fundamental change in thought processes is necessary. We believe that the payoff in better decisions is worth the effort expended. That does not imply that use of risk analysis is a panacea for decision makers.

There is no guarantee that any analysis will foresee all possibilities. "Unique" events have always occurred to spoil "the best laid plans of mice and men." Students of uncertainty in the aerospace community have found it convenient (particularly in presenting testimony to a hostile congress) to partition the states of knowledge into three classes (8), shown in the box below.

The States of Knowledge
1. *Knowns.* Things believed known and already resolved.
2. *Known-unknowns.* Things we know that we don't know. For items in this class it is possible to estimate the uncertainty of events, values, and so on.
3. *Unknown-unknowns (unk-unks).* Things that we don't know we don't know.
Unk-Unks Turn into Flunk-Flunks Aphorism of Rep. Chet Holifield (Calif.)

Conventional analysis deals with only the knowns of the problem. Risk analysis extends the domain of enquiry to include the known-unknowns as well. Nothing short of precognition enables explicit inclusion of the unk-unks.

A Unified Framework for Analysis (The Road Ahead)

In this chapter we have attempted to identify the problem of uncertainty in capital investment analysis, the limitations of conventional approaches, and the concepts and promise of new techniques that explicitly treat uncertainty. Subsequent chapters are designed to elaborate on various aspects of the concepts and techniques. Risk analysis is best viewed in the context of a unified framework for decision making and Figure 1-7 is an attempt at portrayal of the steps in successful problem analysis. To solve problems successfully, it is first necessary to recognize their existence. That has been the subject of Chapter 1. Next, it is necessary to define the objectives of capital investment selection procedures in

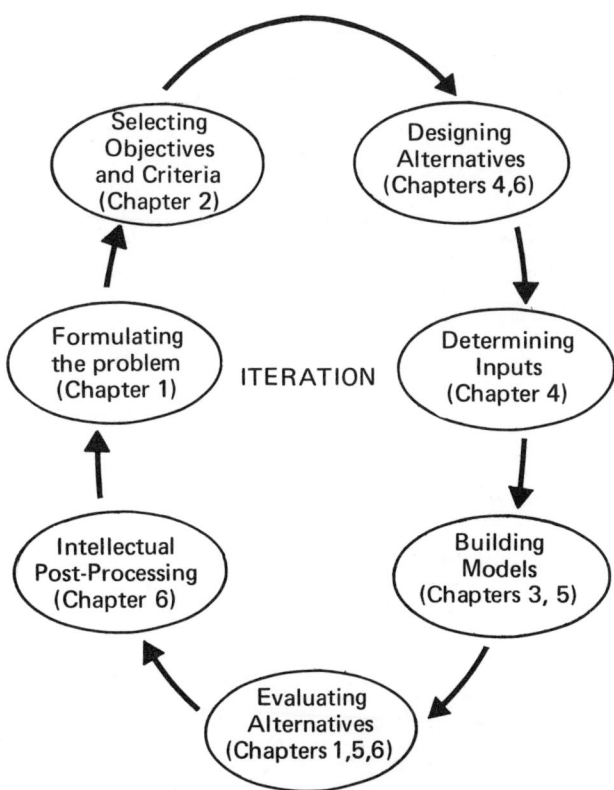

Figure 1-7. A paradigm for successful analysis: Where have we been and where are we going? (Adapted from Quade and Boucher, "Systems Analysis and Policy Planning," American Elsevier Publishing Company, Inc., New York, 1968.)

the light of the objectives of the firm and to identify criteria by which attainment of those objectives can be measured. That is the purpose of Chapter 2. Then alternatives and input must be defined; that process is explored in Chapters 4 and 6. Models can be constructed to determine criterion values from the inputs. Chapters 3 and 5 explore what models are and how they are used. The models can be used to evaluate investment alternatives and form tentative conclusions. Prior to making firm recommendations, we should thoroughly question the assumptions of the analysis and seek to identify better alternatives and inputs. Termed intellectual post-processing (IP^2), that activity is discussed in Chapter 6. Frequently the activity leads to better problem definition. Thus the task of analysis is best described as an iterative process rather than a serial one.

*Good management of capital expenditures
is too vital to be blocked by ignorance,
caution or smugness.*

Joel Dean, in "Measuring the Productivity of Capital,"
Harvard Business Review

2
Selection of Investment Criteria

Viewed in its most general sense, the objective of a capital-budgeting analysis is to weigh the costs of the venture against the benefits that might result from incurring those costs. Though the analysis is simple in concept, it is often difficult in execution.

Take the estimation of benefits as an example. What *is* a benefit? The most obvious determinant is monetary return or profit. Yet there is ample evidence that, even in the absence of uncertainty, firms do not always choose alternatives that maximize monetary returns. Benefits, then, certainly include monetary return but are not limited to it. Qualitative and intangible aspects are also considered. Because of space limitations we will not attempt to address the issue of evaluating collateral and intangible benefits, but the analyst can not afford that omission.

Thus the benefit that we will consider exclusively is monetary return. Even so, we must decide how we will weigh cost against benefit. That is, given a set of alternative investments and their estimated costs and monetary returns, we must devise rules or tests that we can use to *rank* the alternatives, to put them in order of *preference*. The alternatives that appear to contribute the most to company goals will be ranked the highest.

The rules or tests that are used in ranking prospective investments are called *criteria*, and they are the main subject of this chapter. Payback, NPW, and internal rate of return as criteria are described and critiqued. We will argue that NPW—a discounted cash flow procedure—is, when suitably employed, the best criterion to use in capital budgeting. Furthermore, payback period and internal rate of return will be shown to be inadequate and frequently misleading criteria. Those who are familiar with the implications of these criteria are well advised to skip this chapter; those who are not will profit from reading it.

A Description of Some Criteria

When the objective of the firm is to maximize profits, a suitable criterion is that which correctly ranks alternative investments according to their profitability. Many quantities have been proposed as measures of profitability; the following are the better known ones.

1. Payback period (or capital recovery period)
2. Net present worth
3. Internal rate of return

4. Average annual return on initial investment
5. Average annual return on average investment
6. Average annual return on book value of investment
7. MAPI formula
8. Capitalized cost
9. Average annual cost

Measures 4 to 9 will not be discussed here because they have been shown repeatedly to be inadequate and misleading (see Refs. 1, 6, 7, 11, 14). They do not measure profitability. Similarly, payback period does not measure profitability in general. However, payback will be discussed at length in this chapter because of its widespread use—or misuse—as a criterion. Net present worth and internal rate of return are also discussed here, because they *are* meaningful profitability measures.[1]

Estimating After-Tax Cash Flows

All profitability analyses should be based on forecasts of annual cash flows for the life of the investment. Table 2-1 is the profile of an illustrative investment that has a 5-year life and requires an initial outlay of $1,000. The returns shown in the table are net annual cash flows (cash inflow minus cash outflow) *before* depreciation and taxes. However, since profitability is properly measured after taxes, it is necessary to determine the after-tax cash flow. It is calculated for a given year by first subtracting depreciation from before-tax return for that year (column 2 of Table 2-1) and then multiplying the result by 1 minus the tax rate, as shown in columns 3 to 5 of Table 2-2. In our example, the tax rate is assumed to be 52 percent (0.52), and so the multiplier is 1 - 0.52, or 0.48.

Table 2-1. Investment profile.

Year	(1) Investment	(2) Return*
0	1,000	
1		200
2		400
3		600
4		800
5		600

*Return = cash inflow minus cash outflow before depreciation and taxes.

Of course, the resulting *income* is an accounting figure and *not* a cash flow, since depreciation is treated as a cash expense in computing income. However, accounting depreciation is merely a tax shield and is *not* an actual cash expense. Thus, actual after-tax cash flow is computed by adding depreciation back to income, as shown in column 6 of Table 2-2. With the computation of net after-tax cash flows complete, we are in a position to illustrate the definition of payback period.

Definition of Payback Period

The *payback period of an investment* is the amount of time required for the cash proceeds of the investment to pay back the initial outlay. Thus the payback period for our example is between 3 and 4 years, as shown in column 7 of Table 2-2. Discussion and critique of payback period criteria are deferred until later in this chapter; our only purpose at this point is to define payback period.

The Time Value of Money (a Digression)

The two sound profitability measures that we will discuss—net present worth and internal rate of return—are called *discounted cash flow methods*. The methods are used to take explicit account of the *time value* of money in profitability analyses.

Money has a time value for several reasons. One of them is that money received today can be invested at some rate of interest or return and will grow to a larger amount at a later date (assuming that the rate of return is positive). As an illustration, suppose that you deposit $9.25 in a bank today and that interest is paid at 4 percent, compounded annually. If you make no further deposits to it, your account will be worth $9.62 at the end of the first year and $10.00 at the end of the second year, as shown in Figure 2-1.

If we now apply the compound interest logic in reverse, a promise to pay $10.00 to you 2 years from today is worth $9.25 today if you can earn 4 percent interest. In capital budgeting terminology, we would say that the *present value* of $10.00 to be received 2 years from today is $9.25, again if you are able to invest at 4 percent interest. The process of determining the present value of a future amount is called *discounting*. The rate of interest that can be earned on available money is called the *discount rate*.

The Definition of Net Present Worth

Imagine now an investment that has a 2-year life and net after-tax cash flows of $9.62 in the first year and $10.00 (additional) in the second year. The total cash flow for the investment over its entire life is $19.62.

---
[1] However, subsequent discussion will show that internal rate of return can be properly applied to a much narrower range of problems than net present worth.

Table 2-2. Cash flow analysis.

Year	(1) Investment	(2) Return	(3) Depreciation	(4) Before-Tax Income (2) - (3)	(5) After-Tax Income 0.48 [(2) - (3)]	(6) Cash Flow (5) + (3)	(7) Accumulated Cash Flow
0	1,000					−1,000	−1,000
1		200	200	0	0	200	− 800
2		400	200	200	96	296	− 504
3		600	200	400	192	392	− 112
4		800	200	600	288	488	+ 376 ← Payback
5		600	200	300	144	344	+ 720

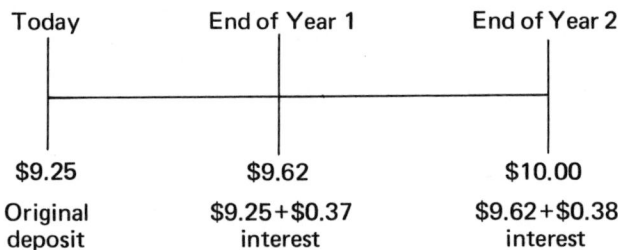

Figure 2-1. An illustration of compound interest.

Table 2-4. Computing the net present worth of an investment.

Year	Investment	Net Cash Flow	Present Value of Net Cash Flow at 4%
0	$17.00		
1		$ 9.62	$ 9.25
2		10.00	9.25
Total	$17.00		$18.50

NPW = $18.50 − 17.00 = $1.50

Would you then pay $19.62 today to purchase that series of cash flows? The answer depends on your alternative uses of money. Specifically, if your best alternative to the investment were to deposit your money in a bank at 4 percent, then you would be willing to pay $18.50 for the investment, assuming that it has the same risk as the bank deposit. The reason, shown in Table 2-3, is that the present value of the series of cash flows from the investment is $18.50 if the discount rate is 4 percent. That is, $18.50 deposited today at 4 percent will have increased to $19.62 at the end of 2 years.

Table 2-3. An illustration of present value.

Year	Net Cash Flow	Present Value of Net Cash Flow at 4%
1	$ 9.62	$ 9.25
2	10.00	9.25
Total	$19.62	$18.50

Finally we compute the NPW of the investment if the initial outlay is known. Suppose that the outlay was $17.00; then the NPW of the investment is $1.50 ($18.50 − 17.00), as shown in Table 2-4. That means you could pay an additional $1.50 (over and above the $17.00) for the investment and still earn the required 4 percent. Of course, a negative NPW would mean that the investment would *not* earn the required rate of return.

Procedures identical with those described here are used in measuring the profitability of real capital investments. Whereas the discount rate was 4 percent for the preceding illustration, in actuality the firm must specify the discount rate to use in computing NPW. The appropriate discount rate for a firm is its *cost of capital*. Some authorities maintain that the cost of capital is the weighted average of all capital sources (equity and long- and short-term debt), which is currently about 10 percent for most firms. Others, particularly economists, say that the cost of capital is an *opportunity* cost; that is, the cost of opportunities foregone by accepting a particular investment.

In any case, assume for illustrative purposes that the firm's cost of capital is 15 percent. Then the NPW of the investment discussed earlier in this chapter is $106, as shown in column 10 of Table 2-5. The *discount factors* shown in column 9 of the table are the present values of $1 at 15 percent for the appropriate years.

If the firm's cost of capital were 20 percent, then the NPW of the investment would be −$28; that is, the investment would earn less than the firm's cost of capital.

The Definition of Internal Rate of Return

Internal rate of return (IRR), a concept related to net present worth, is the true annual rate of return earned by an investment. It is defined as the discount rate that yields an NPW of zero, that is, the rate of interest that equates the present value of cash flows to the initial outlay.

As Table 2-5 shows, the IRR is calculated by trial and error. At a 15 percent discount rate NPW is positive, and at a 20 percent rate it is negative. Since the IRR is the discount rate that results in an NPW of zero, it must

Table 2-5. Complete investment analysis.

Year	(1) Investment	(2) Return	(3) Depreciation	(4) Before-Tax Income (2) − (3)	(5) After-Tax Income 0.48 [(2) − (3)]	(6) Cash Flow (5) + (3)	(7) Accumulated Cash Flow
0	1,000					−1,000	−1,000
1		200	200	0	0	200	− 800
2		400	200	200	96	296	− 504
3		600	200	400	192	392	− 112
4		800	200	600	288	488	+ 376 ← Payback
5		600	200	300	144	344	+ 720

Year	(8) Cash Flow ($)	(9) Discount Factor at 15%	(10) Present Worth ($)	(11) Discount Factor at 20%	(12) Present Worth ($)	(13) Discount Factor at 19%	(14) Present Worth ($)
0	−1,000	1.000	−1,000	1.000	−1,000	1.000	−1,000
1	200	0.869	174	0.833	167	0.840	168
2	296	0.756	224	0.694	205	0.706	209
3	392	0.658	258	0.579	227	0.593	232
4	488	0.572	279	0.482	235	0.499	244
5	344	0.497	171	0.402	138	0.419	144
			106		− 28		− 3

lie between 15 and 20 percent. At a discount rate of 19 percent, NPW is -$3, or approximately zero. Thus, the IRR for the investment illustrated in Table 2-5 is approximately 19 percent. The relationship between IRR and NPW is illustrated graphically in Figure 2-2.

Figure 2-2. Relationship between NPW and IRR.

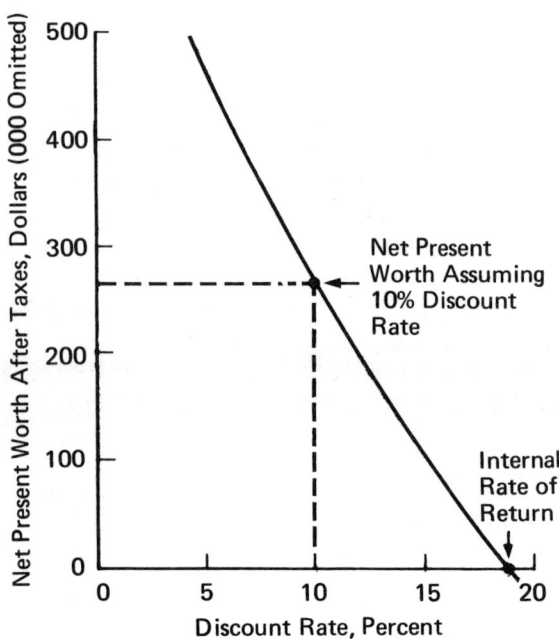

We turn now to a discussion of the advantages and limitations of payback period, NPW, and IRR as measures of profitability. The discussion of payback comes first.

The Payback Criterion: A Critical Appraisal

As stated earlier, the payback period is the number of years required for the cash proceeds from an investment to pay back the initial outlay. According to the most commonly followed payback rule, investments with payback periods of x years or greater should be rejected, and those with payback periods of fewer than x years should be accepted. The maximum acceptable payback period, or x, for most firms is 2 to 8 years, and it is determined by experience. The specific period will generally depend on the kind of project, the type of financing, the state of the company, and so forth.

Payback is extremely popular as an investment criterion. For instance, Christy (4), in a 1964 survey of 108 firms, reported that:

> A maximum payback period was the most popular form of standard used.... Lagging badly in [last] place came the discounted cash flow procedures... so heavily favored by academic writers on capital budgeting.

The popularity of payback as a criterion is due in large measure to claims that payback is a good measure of liquidity, an acceptable measure of profitability, and a good measure of risk and is easy to calculate and easy to understand. Some of these claims are fairly accurate in specific instances; others are totally false. In general, however, acceptance of the claims can lead and has led to dangerous conclusions, as indicated in later sections.

Payback as an Easy-to-Use Tool

There is little doubt that payback period is easily computed and understood, but in any discussion of payback as an investment criterion it is necessary to recall that a maximum acceptable period must be stated, generally on the basis of "experience." That value is generally difficult or impossible to determine rationally. Payback period is certainly easy to use, but, as Herbert Dougall (8) aptly points out, "Perhaps this is a real *defect* of the test. Its very simplicity may lead to illogical use."

Payback as a Liquidity Measure

Payback period is often a useful measure of liquidity to the extent that shorter payback periods mean more rapid accumulation of cash proceeds. Consequently, cash-hungry firms often use payback as a rough screening device where liquidity considerations are paramount. Nonetheless, payback period is frequently misleading even in a liquidity sense. For example, Table 2-6 shows two investments that have identical payback periods. Are they therefore identical from a liquidity standpoint? Clearly, the answer is no. Investment 2 pays back 50 percent of the initial outlay after one year; whereas 5 years is required for investment 1 to pay back that percent. Thus, a display of percent payback by year for each investment would be superior to payback period as a liquidity measure.

The Table 2-6 illustration is admittedly contrived to make a point, but don't let that mislead you. Actual cash flow comparisons such as the comparison of the table are not uncommon. Furthermore, cash flow projections are frequently omitted from payback presentations, which renders direct cash flow comparisons impossible.

To summarize, the payback period may be too gross a liquidity measure depending, of course, upon specific circumstances.

Payback as a Profitability Measure

The statement that payback period is a measure of relative profitability of investment opportunities is generally inaccurate. In fact, payback is a meaningful profitability measure *solely* for investments that have uniform cash flows for their entire economic lives and that have long economic lives as well. Moreover, payback measures profitability for those kinds of projects only because the reciprocal of payback is a good approximation to the IRR *in those cases.*

Many practitioners believe, however, that payback is a good measure of profitability in general. They argue that the life of an investment after payback is an indicator of investment profitability. Thus the argument continues, payback period is a good profitability measure for projects that have roughly identical economic lives. To see why that kind of reasoning can be dangerous, it is only necessary to consider some of the shortcomings of payback as a criterion.

1. Payback period ignores the economic life of an investment. Since explicit estimation of economic life is not a part of payback procedures, it is unlikely that decision makers who use payback to measure profitability would actually know whether investments have "roughly identical lives" or not.

Also, and probably of greater importance, the payback calculation, in its disregard of economic life, ignores cash flows beyond the payback period. Payback advocates dismiss that deficiency with the argument that cash flow forecasts beyond payback are generally so uncertain as to be worthless anyway. This argument may have been substantive at one time, but it is patently untrue in the context of risk analysis.

2. The payback calculation ignores or disguises the shapes of cash flow streams. If the timing of cash flows were not a relevant factor in capital budgeting, then the criticism would have less weight. However, cash flow timing is important from a profitability point of view because money has a time value.

3. The relationship between maximum acceptable payback period and profitability is unclear. As an example, consider a firm that has a maximum acceptable payback period of 2 years for cost reduction proposals. Suppose that the firm has the option of undertaking a machine-replacement program. The initial outlay re-

Table 2-6. Two investments with identical payback periods.

Investment	Initial Outlay ($)	Net Cash Flow ($) in Year						Payback Period Years
		1	2	3	4	5	6	
1	60,000	2,000	3,000	5,000	7,000	13,000	30,000	6
2	60,000	30,000	13,000	7,000	5,000	3,000	2,000	6

quired is $40,000, and the projected cost savings are $10,000 annually for the next 7 years if the project is undertaken today. By application of the 2-year payback rule, the project would be rejected, because project payback is estimated to be 4 years.

Imagine now that profitability was the controlling factor in the machine-replacement decision. Does the payback criterion measure profitability? Interestingly enough, that question cannot even be addressed without resorting to the use of other, and better, profitability measures. The true (internal) return on investment for the machine-replacement project is 16 percent. Now, rejection of the project according to the payback test may, by chance, be a sensible decision *if* the firm can invest the $40,000 elsewhere at a return greater than 16 percent.

Consider as well a second implication of payback as an investment criterion in this example. The machine-replacement project would be delayed until projected cost savings were $20,000 annually. If there is rhyme or reason to such a decision, it would appear to be the result of forces that are not well understood by mere mortals.

Payback as a Measure of Risk

As in the case of liquidity and profitability, the advocacy of using payback to measure risk must be hedged by suitable disclaimers. Many writers on capital budgeting have neglected to hedge, however. For instance, Herbert Dougall (8), in an article entitled "Payback as an Aid in Capital Budgeting" states, "Of course, the shorter the actual payback time, the less risk associated with a particular project." Joel Dean (7) at least adds some qualifications in asserting that "[payback period] can be useful for appraising risky investments where the rate of capital wastage is particularly hard to predict." Overall, though, the statement that shorter payback means less risk needs considerable clarification and qualification.

One source of confusion is illustrated in Table 2-7, which shows two proposed investments. Investment 1 has a 6-year payback period; investment 2 has a 2-year payback. Does it necessarily follow that investment 1 is riskier than investment 2? The answer is No it does not. Closer scrutiny reveals why. Investment 1 is a cost reduction effort; investment 2 is a new product introduction. Generally, new product introductions are far more risky than cost reduction efforts. Bower (2) has presented some interesting evidence to substantiate that claim (as though more evidence were necessary). He found that, on the average, the actual profitability of new product introductions has been only 10 percent of the predicted values. In contrast, predictions of the profitability of cost reduction efforts were extremely accurate. Consequently, when the investments compared are such as those shown in Table 2-7, risk-ranking on the basis of payback is not advisable.

Some practitioners believe that the shortcomings of situations such as the one described here are easily rectified by using qualitative *risk classes*. In one such procedure, projects are classified as low, medium, or high risk and the payback period is then used as a measure of risk only for projects in the same risk class.

Although risk classification procedures do render the use of payback period as a measure of risk more rational, shortcomings persist. Consider, as an illustration, two investments that are in the same risk class, as shown in Table 2-8. They have identical payback periods. Have they, therefore, identical risks? In general, the answer is maybe. Specifically, it is wise to note first that the cash flows for investment 1 increase over time, whereas those for investment 2 decline. If the uncertainty in cash flows increases over time, as it often does, then investment 1 may be much more risky than investment 2; major cash flows for it occur relatively far out in time. Thus payback period will, in general, be inadequate as a risk measure unless projects are categorized qualitatively according to the level of risk and the stream of cash flows is "visible."

Finally, let us suppose that payback does actually measure risk. Even so, the net result is a relative risk measure, not an absolute one. Thus we may determine that A is more risky than B and yet have no idea how risky either one is, unless in a low-medium-high sense. When we recognize that one man's high is another's low, we begin to see the magnitude of the problem.

In summary, payback is popular but not powerful. It yields gross, and often misleading, estimates of many things, but accurate measures of nothing. Perhaps the biggest factor in the payback popularity story is that many managers prefer projects with short payback periods because the shorter the payback period, the sooner profitability will be visible (16).

Table 2-7. The use of payback period in measuring risk.

Investment	Initial Outlay ($)	Net Cash Flow ($) in Year						Payback Period Years
		1	2	3	4	5	6	
1. Cost reduction	60,000	30,000	13,000	7,000	5,000	3,000	2,000	6
2. New product introduction	60,000	30,000	30,000	30,000	30,000	30,000	30,000	2

Table 2-8. Two investments in the same risk class.

Investment	Initial Outlay ($)	Net Cash Flow ($) in Year						Payback Period Years
		1	2	3	4	5	6	
1. Cost reduction	60,000	2,000	3,000	5,000	7,000	13,000	30,000	6
2. Cost reduction	60,000	30,000	13,000	7,000	5,000	3,000	2,000	6

Net Present Worth: Advantages and Limitations

Net present worth, a discounted cash flow technique, is a sound profitability measure. The NPW for an investment is defined as the present value of the stream of net flows for the project minus the initial cash outlay. Phrased somewhat differently, NPW is the present value of cash inflows minus the present value of cash outflows. The present value of a stream of cash flows is computed by using some specific rate of interest. The interest or discount rate used is properly the firm's *cost of capital.* NPW calculations are illustrated in Table 2-5.

To recapitulate what was said earlier in this chapter, if the NPW of a project is zero, then the firm's return on investment is identical with its cost of capital. NPW values less than zero mean that the firm's return on investment is less than its cost of capital; conversely, NPW values greater than zero mean that return exceeds the cost of capital. Suppose, for example, that the NPW of a project is estimated to be $20,000. That amount can be interpreted as the premium that a firm could pay for the investment today and still earn its required return on investment.

The NPW rule involves a ranking of alternatives according to their profitability as follows: Accept all projects that have a net present worth greater than zero. If not all such projects can be accepted (because of funding limitations, for example), select those with the highest NPW. Bear in mind that profitability is the sole concern here but that other relevant factors, whether tangible or intangible, must be considered in the final decisions. The following are some of the advantages of NPW:

1. NPW takes explicit account of the time value of money, the economic life of the project, and the firm's cost of capital.

2. Although NPW measures profitability only, useful measures of liquidity (including payback period) are derived from the inputs to NPW analysis.

3. When coupled with risk analysis techniques, NPW becomes an explicit measure of profitability risk as well as a measure of profitability.

4. If risk analysis techniques are used, then useful measures of liquidity risk can also be readily derived from the inputs to NPW risk computations.

Net present worth has the minor disadvantage that it is more difficult to calculate than payback period, but it is easier to calculate than discounted cash flow rate of return (see Table 2-5). In any case, canned computer programs are available for making the calculation. Moreover, the risk analysis techniques described in this briefing are computer-based. Thus the requirement for computer-assisted NPW calculations is irrelevant if risk analysis is used.

Discussion of Arguments Against NPW

1. Bower (2) argues that NPW is unsound on "theoretical" grounds "because it ignores the essential effects of uncertainty." In other words, Bower maintains that cash flow forecasts for different projects are not comparable because of uncertainties. The argument is sound but *misdirected.* Its true thrust is against *the use of deterministic analyses* and not against NPW.

2. Some practitioners argue that the firm cannot determine its cost of capital. Although that argument is difficult to answer directly and generally, it does appear that rational choices concerning required profitability would be rather difficult in the absence of knowledge of a breakeven profitability level.

3. Some firms are wary of discounted cash flow techniques, or, more specifically, of systematic planning techniques, because they fear that that approach to planning may lead to overcentralization and usurpation of line functions by staff planners. The issue cannot be resolved in this briefing if, for that matter, it could be resolved in any book of considerable length.

4. Lerner and Rappaport (13) point out that NPW criteria ignore the timing of cash flows and that indiscriminate use of NPW may result in an earnings stream that looks "bad" to stockholders. That is a valid argument in some cases, and it is one that demonstrates the need to recognize the timing of cash flows explicitly and treat it in investment analysis.

As an illustration of the point, consider a firm that acquires capital solely from equity. Assume that the firm's common stock currently has a price-earnings ratio of 20:1; then the firm's cost of capital is 5 percent.[2] Now imagine that the firm's stream of earnings for the next 4 years were to look like this:

Year	1	2	3	4
Earnings ($mm)	4.7	2.1	6.1	3.4

The variability in cash flow would affect the perceived utility of the firm's stock to the investor, and the stock price might then fall. A decrease in the stock price would lower the price-earnings ratio and thereby increase the firm's cost of capital.

Thus, when maximizing NPW might result in an erratic earnings stream, other criteria would be useful. They might involve minimizing the firm's cost of capital or maximizing investor utility. Although little work has been done in this area to date, recent advances have been made in applying quantitative techniques to the problem.[3]

Concluding Remarks on NPW

Net present worth is a sound and readily usable measure of profitability. When maximization of NPW would result in an erratic stream of earnings, some modification of the NPW criterion would be necessary.

Internal Rate of Return: Advantages and Limitations

As indicated earlier, the IRR of an investment is the discount rate at which the NPW of the investment is zero. The method of calculation and the interpretation of the measure is illustrated in Table 2-5 and Figure 2-2.

Internal rate of return has many of the same advantages as NPW. In addition, the measure itself is somewhat easier to interpret than NPW. A further "perceived advantage" is that IRR can be computed without explicitly determining the firm's cost of capital. However that advantage quickly vanishes when the firm must decide upon the "hurdle rate" or minimum acceptable rate of return.

However, the IRR has some very definite limitations, the consequence of which is that the measure is useful in only a limited number of applications.

[2] Some (1) maintain that the cost of capital to a firm that acquires capital solely from equity is related to the current *price-dividends ratio* and the expected annual rate of increase in dividends. And, of course, if capital is acquired from both debt and equity, then the cost of capital will be a weighted average of the cost of acquiring each kind of capital.

[3] The most outstanding result of this work to date is the MUM (maxim utility model).

1. The assumption is that cash throw-offs from a project are reinvested at the IRR. Thus, if the predicted rate of return is, say, 50 percent, the assumption is that all cash throw-offs from the project will be reinvested at 50 percent. That will be patently untrue in specific cases.

2. Projects with irregular net cash flow patterns over time (for example, --+++--) may have multiple rates of return; alternatively, a rate of return may not exist. Thus, for example, a project that shows negative cash flows for the first 3 years, positive cash flows for the next 2 years, and negative cash flows thereafter may have internal rates of return of, say, 12 and 34 percent or no rate of return at all. For a thorough discussion of the topic, see Bierman and Smidt (1).

3. The IRR may not be meaningful for small initial outlays. In the extreme case, a project that requires no initial outlay at all has an infinite rate of return. The result for a project that requires a small nonzero initial outlay but may commit the firm to a substantial future outlay may be equally meaningless. Of course, the difficulty of defining "small" further complicates the matter.

4. Mutually exclusive projects that require different initial outlays or have different economic lives are very difficult to compare by using IRR. That is a particularly severe restriction of IRR as an investment criterion. It has led to misuse in comparing competitive projects only one of which may be accepted, because the shortcomings of the criterion in this respect are not obvious to most people. Bierman and Smidt (1) treat this subject well.

The assumptions underlying IRR are sufficient cause to rule it out in general except as a supplement to the use of NPW. However, when the assumptions that underlie it are valid, IRR can be a very useful and sound measure of profitability.

In addition, IRR is compatible with the risk analysis techniques described in this briefing. If IRR is used as a criterion, risk analysis is a far better method of handling uncertainties than such intuitive procedures as increasing the required rate of return, or the hurdle rate for risky projects.

Summary

Risk analysis will be wasted effort if inappropriate investment criteria are used. Net present worth is clearly the best of available choices of criteria. Other investment criteria, such as payback period and IRR, are inadequate and are often misleading.

Net present worth is a measure of profitability only. Since most firms have many objectives and constraints and many intangible factors operating in capital budgeting, the indiscriminate use of *any* single criterion is inadvisable.

Until recently, investment analyses have been characterized by one major weakness. Cash flows for all years in the life of all investments have been treated as though they were forecast with equal certainty. Thus cash flows for later years were weighted equally with those for earlier years, at least from the standpoint of uncertainty. That shortcoming is avoided by the use of risk analysis, whereby cash flow uncertainties are an explicit (that is, quantitative) part of the cash flow forecasts.

By application of risk analysis procedures, NPW becomes an objective measure of *profitability risk* as well as a measure of *profitability* per se. Moreover, sound and objective measures of *liquidity and liquidity risk* are trivially derived from risk analysis inputs.

Overall, the use of NPW coupled with risk analysis is an extremely powerful, if somewhat new and unfamiliar, procedure. Given time and the demands of business, we believe that the procedure will be instituted on a large scale.

The tools ... available to the analyst, planner, and decision maker ... are many times better than anything we have had before. It is just barely possible that with determined efforts by large numbers of responsible people we can achieve enough to make a significant difference.

Herman Kahn
On Thermonuclear War

3
Mathematical Tools For Risk Analysis

Quantitative risk analysis of financial alternatives would be impossible were it not for three important developments since the 1930s. The first was the application of scientific method to business problems, as manifested primarily by the use of *mathematical models*. A mathematical model is merely a mathematical *equation* ($A = B + C$ is an example) that relates some quantity of interest such as NPW to various "explanatory" variables such as share of market, selling price, and operating costs.

Second, chronologically, was the systematic development of Monte Carlo *simulation* methods by Harris and Kahn in 1948. By use of those methods, mathematical equations that include uncertainty can be solved explicitly and thus quantitatively. Although its original applications were to atomic physics, simulation became an indispensable business tool during the sixties.

Finally, the concept of subjective probability—reintroduced by Leonard Savage (8) in the mid-fifties and popularized in the sixties—made possible the application of mathematical modeling and simulation to a host of business problems that had previously been considered not to be amenable to that application. Subjective probability is simply an individual's "quantified intuition" concerning the likelihood that an event of interest will occur.

The roles of modeling, probability, and simulation in risk analysis can be summarized as follows. When we model an investment, we define the relevant variables and their interrelationship with the measures of investment worth. We then quantify the uncertainties in the numerical values of the variables in the models by an application of subjective probability. Finally, we derive the probability distribution of the measures of investment worth via the process of simulation.

The mechanics of modeling, probability theory, and simulation are properly the concern of analysts, but decision makers must understand the logic and terminology of those tools if they are to utilize the results of financial risk analyses correctly and effectively.

Models

A model is an abstraction or representation of some real thing. There are three kinds of models in common use:

1. *Iconic models,* which look like the real thing. Examples include pilot chemical plants and wind tunnel airplane models.

2. *Analog models,* which use one quantity to represent another. A relief map wherein color represents elevation is an analog model of real terrain. Analog models are more abstract than iconic models.

3. *Symbolic* or *mathematical models,* which use symbols (*A, B, X, Y,* and so on) to represent real quantities. Since the symbols do not resemble the real quantities in any way, mathematical models are a totally abstract representation of reality. The abstraction leads to some important advantages and limitations, as we shall see subsequently.

Each of the three types of models—iconic, analog, and mathematical—is used extensively in business and industry. However, mathematical models are of special interest here because their formulation and use are necessary in risk analysis. We will be concerned with mathematical models exclusively in ensuing discussions.

Uses of Mathematical Models

To repeat, mathematical models are simply mathematical equations used in financial analysis for *optimization* and *prediction*. Optimization models are used as an aid to determining so-called optimal courses of action in which, as Fabian (2) has pointed out:

> Either the number of decision variables [is] so immense that the human mind is incapable of reviewing even a small percent of all available decision alternatives or the decision problems [are] too complex for the unaided human mind to see through the tangled web of interactions between the variables and to resolve what the optimum course of action should be.

Some of the best known optimization models are the linear programming ones used to determine production and distribution schedules that satisfy customer demand and other constraints at minimum cost or maximum profit. In recent years, many useful optimization models have been formulated for application to financial analysis. Since space limitations prohibit discussion of those models here, the interested reader should consult Refs. 4 to 6.

Predictive models are used as an aid to forecasting or estimating such future quantities as fixed and operating costs and market growth rate of a proposed capital investment. Predictive mathematical models are valuable because model-derived estimates are generally *more accurate* than other estimates. That point is illustrated in the next section.

Improved Accuracy from Predictive Models

There are two basic approaches to dealing with the uncertainties that characterize all financial problems:

1. *Ignore them.* Those who feel comfortable using rules of thumb for decision making follow this approach.

2. *Recognize and attempt to reduce uncertainties.* Insurance, hedging, and mathematical models are but a few of the tools available for the reduction of uncertainty.

To appreciate the use of a mathematical model to reduce uncertainty, work through the following "convince yourself" exercise. Begin by estimating the volume of the pyramid shown full-size in Figure 3-1. All the sides of the pyramid are the same length. Simply take a guess at the volume in cubic inches and record your guess in the space provided.

Figure 3-1. What is the estimated volume of the pyramid?

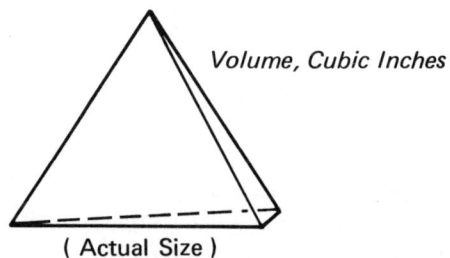

As you have probably discovered, it is difficult to think in terms of volume directly. In fact, most of us will have resorted to the following two-step procedure for estimating the pyramid volume:

1. Estimate the length of a side.
2. Try to deduce the *relationship* between the length of a side and the volume of the pyramid. (Estimating pyramid volume as a percent of the volume of a cube

with sides equal to the pyramid sides is merely a clever way to estimate that relationship, since we know the relationship between side length and volume for a cube.)

Thus there are two major sources of uncertainty—or error—in the prediction of pyramid volume: uncertainty concerning the length of a side and uncertainty concerning the relationship between side length and volume. We can improve predictive accuracy by reducing or eliminating either or both of the sources of uncertainty. The power of a predictive mathematical model is that it reduces or eliminates the second source of uncertainty, the relationship between side length and volume. You can prove that to yourself by estimating the volume of the pyramid again. This time, however, use the mathematical model

$$V \cong 0.12 L^3$$

in which V represents volume and L represents length. Now you can estimate volume by estimating only side length directly and deriving your volume estimate from the model. Space for your calculations is provided in Figure 3-2.

Figure 3-2. What is the calculated volume of the pyramid?

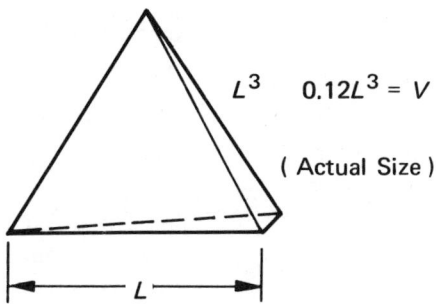

Your second estimate is probably more accurate than your first. Judge for yourself. The true volume of the pyramid is 0.234 cubic inches.

The value of predictive mathematical models in financial analysis becomes apparent when we recognize that such measures as return on investment, NPW, and share of the market are analogous to volume of the pyramid: they are difficult to understand and estimate *directly*. Greater predictive accuracy is possible by use of mathematical models because, *by design*, the variables in a mathematical model are easier to estimate than the actual quantities of interest. Moreover, the model allows us to determine the effect of errors in the variables on the quantities of interest. In the pyramid example each error of 10 percent in length of a side will result in a 33 percent error in volume. That is an example of a technique called sensitivity analysis, which is treated in Chapter 6.

An Illustrative Capital Investment Model

Mathematical modeling is more an art than a science. The "art" consists largely in determining the optimal level of detail for the variables. In the pyramid example, volume is too gross a measure to be estimated directly. On the other hand, we could say that volume of the pyramid is related to the length D of the line

by

$$V = 5.5 D^4$$

That level of detail is too great, since it is difficult to estimate the length of so short a line accurately. In general, then, the process of modeling starts at very gross or high levels. The model is then made more detailed, as necessary, until the optimal level of detail is reached.

As an illustration, consider the following mathematical model. It is to be used as an aid to predicting the NPW of a proposed investment.

$$\text{NPW} = \sum_{t=1}^{N} \frac{CF_t}{(1+r)^t}$$

where NPW = net present worth, dollars
N = economic life of investment, years
r = cost of capital or discount rate, decimal
CF_t = net cash flow in year t, dollars

Note, in the model, that the variables—economic life, cost of capital, and yearly net cash flows—are easier to understand and estimate than NPW is. (Of course, that does not imply absolute ease in estimation of the variables; it implies merely relative ease.) Note, however, that yearly net cash flow can itself be related to still other variables. In the following mathematical model for yearly net cash flows, the variables—tax rate, yearly operating expenses and so on—are easier to understand and estimate than cash flows.

$$CF_t = (1 - TR)(R_t - OE_t) + TR(D_t)$$

where CF_t = after-tax net cash flow in year t, dollars
TR = tax rate, decimal
R_t = gross revenue in year t, dollars
OE_t = operating expenses in year t, dollars
D_t = depreciation reserve in year t, dollars

As you have no doubt deduced by now, the process of modeling might, in a new product introduction, for example, continue by relating revenues to share of market, total market, and selling price. Operating expense might be related to fixed and variable costs and so forth. Again, the good analyst will know where to stop. He must understand the implication of the trade-off between detail, or realism, and usefulness of the model. That aspect of modeling is discussed in the next section.

Relevance in Models

Good models are, *by design,* simpler and easier to understand than the reality that they represent. That is because good models include *only* those factors that are *relevant* to the decision at hand.

If, for example, you are planning to drive from Princeton to Newark and must select a route, a road map is a model that includes the factors relevant to your decision.(7) But if you are a highway planner and must determine the route for a new superhighway between Princeton and Newark, then a road map is not an adequate model. It excludes factors relevant to your decision. You need topographic maps, detailed urban maps, maps of land value, and so forth. It is important to note also, however, that very detailed maps are of *less* value to you in the first instance than a simple road map. Why? Because they include factors that are *irrelevant* to your decision as a motorist. They *needlessly* complicate the situation.

As in maps, so too in mathematical models. Too much detail is often as bad as too little. In fact, in making their case for the use of simple models, Enthoven and Smith (1) note that:

> Far too many . . . studies are so complex that they are hardly understood by anyone except (and sometimes including) their authors. The most compelling reason to make analyses understandable is to make them useful to decision makers. We all recognize that decision makers usually add judgment to the facts they consider. This is as it should be. . . . However, in cases where the decision maker does not personally understand at least the basic logic of the analysis, he may be forced to rely on judgment entirely. . . . [Few] would argue that this is a desirable situation.

Experience bears witness to the accuracy of the preceding statement. Decision makers do commonly reject models because they are too complicated (and often unnecessarily so). However, some of the same decision makers and many analysts reject simple models on the ground that they are "unrealistic." That is unfortunate, if the models include all relevant factors, since

> The object of the model is not to imitate for the sake of imitation, but to enable certain decisions to be taken; and the question is whether what we omit in a simplified model is relevant to the decision, not to the accuracy of the representation. (3)

Therein lies a very fundamental and serious problem with regard to modeling. Analysts frequently substitute unnecessarily complex models for adequate simple ones because "simple models are too rough and inaccurate." On the other hand, decision makers frequently substitute unaided judgment for simple models that they reject because of "unrealism." Alain Enthoven used to have a sign in his office in defense of simple models. It read:

**It's Better to Be Roughly Right
than Exactly Wrong**

The Mathematics of Uncertainty

The branch of mathematics that is used to derive, manipulate, and display information about *uncertain* quantities is called *probability theory.* An example of an uncertain quantity is the total U.S. market for new cars in 1978.

Probabilistic concepts are central to the process of risk analysis. They are used in determining inputs to the analysis and in display of outputs. Even the mechanisms for solving risk analysis models are probabilistic. Here our main concern with probability has to do with the various kinds of displays of probabilistic information. Before we proceed, however, it will be necessary to know the meaning of "probability."

The Meaning of Probability

Two definitions of probability are in common use today. By the first and better known one, probability is a long-term regularity that underlies random events. For example, the outcome of one toss of a fair coin is uncertain, but we expect that heads will appear about half the time in the long run—that is, after a very large number of tosses. In this case, we would say that the probability that heads will occur on any one toss is 0.5, or one-half.

The concept of probability as relative frequency in the long run underlies such diverse subjects as statistical quality control, Gallup polls, and life insurance rates. Moreover, it is the stuff and substance of Edward Thorp's winning strategy for blackjack[1] and a proven method for beating the horses. The following are the salient features of this kind of probability:

1. The element of repeatability. (The coin can be tossed repeatedly.)
2. The fact that probability estimates are derived from empirical, or "hard," data.

Those two features do not, however, characterize *subjective probability*, which is the second type and the one most frequently used in financial risk analysis. Subjective probability estimates are *not* formally derived from empirical data, nor need the events of interest be repeatable. Instead subjective probability is simply an individual's "quantified judgment" of the likelihood of occurrence of some event of interest. Therefore, instead of expressing qualitative likelihood judgments ("It's pretty likely that the total market will exceed 8 million cars."), the individual now quantifies his judgment ("There's an 85 percent chance that the total market will exceed 8 million cars.").[2]

Quantification of judgment opens the door to the application of powerful mathematical tools to knotty problems of uncertainty. True, the costs of obtaining and manipulating the necessary subjective probability estimates are greater than the evident costs of ignoring uncertainty or treating it qualitatively. However, our experience suggests that the benefits derived from such procedures far outweigh the costs. What benefits can we expect? The next section answers that question.

Probabilistic Information Portrayal

Earlier we claimed that probability theory can be used to great advantage in portraying all available information about uncertain quantities. Two general formats are used to that end: graphical displays and summary statistics. Graphical displays convey information concerning the *range* and *likelihood* of possible values of an uncertain quantity. Summary statistics convey various subsets of the information presented in the graphical displays. We will use the uncertain quantity "total U.S. market for new cars in 1978" as a vehicle for discussion of data displays.

---

[1] If you read this footnote, then you are more interested in card games than financial risk analysis. Please go now; read Thorp's *Beat the Dealer: A Winning Strategy for the Game of Twenty-One* (New York: Vintage Books, Random House, Inc., 1966) and return here with unfettered mind.

[2] Recommended methods for eliciting subjective probability estimates are discussed in Chapter 4, "Obtaining Inputs to a Risk Analysis."

Imagine, for the sake of argument, that the 1978 total U.S. market could conceivably be as low as 5 million new cars or as high as 11 million. Although it is a simple matter to specify that range, the task of specifying the likelihood of occurrence of all possible values in the range is more complex, since there are 6 million possible values. It is more practical to provide likelihood information for groups or intervals of possible values than for individual values. Table 3-1 shows an example of that means of specifying likelihood data. The selection of the width and number of intervals in Table 3-1 is somewhat arbitrary. One consideration in the selection is that all values within a given interval are assumed to be *equally likely* to occur. Thus, in the new car example, a 5.1-million market is assumed to be as likely as a 6.9-million market. If that is too gross a representation, narrower intervals may be necessary. However, there are limits to the narrowness of the intervals, a matter that is discussed in subsequent sections.

Table 3-1. An easy way to describe the total U.S. market for new cars in 1978.

Range of Values for Total Car Market (Millions)	Probability That Total Market Will Fall Within the Specified Range
5–7	0.15
7–8	0.10
8–9	0.30
9–10	0.35
10–11	0.10

Histogram Representation

The information in Table 3-1 can also be displayed graphically, as in Figure 3-3, in a format called a *histogram*. Probability is represented by the *area* of the bars in the histogram rather than by bar height. Thus the area of the leftmost bar in Figure 3-3 represents the probability that total market will be between 5 and 7 million cars. Although that probability is greater than the one for the 7- to 8-million interval, the bar for the latter interval is higher. That merely illustrates the cautionary remark that area, not height, denotes probability in a histogram.

The total area under a histogram is unity, since it is a certainty (the probability is 1) that the value of the random variable will lie within the range shown on the horizontal axis. That facilitates visual interpretation as follows. The probability associated with any combination of histogram intervals is identical with the fraction, or percent, of total histogram area that is accounted for

Figure 3-3. An illustrative histogram for the total U.S. market for new cars in 1978.

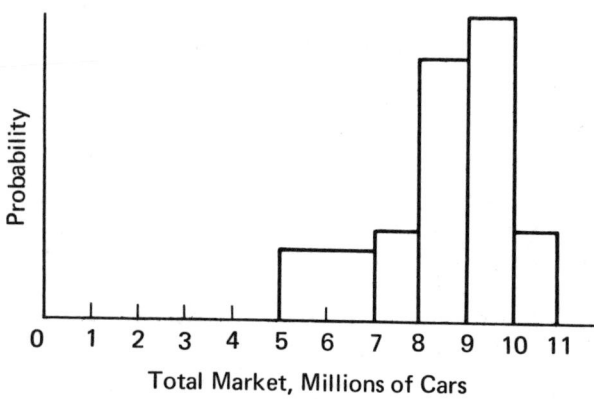

by the intervals of interest. To take a simple case, the probability that the random variable of Figure 3-4 will be less than zero is 50 percent. That is, half of the total histogram area lies to the left of zero.

Figure 3-4. An example of visual probability assessment.

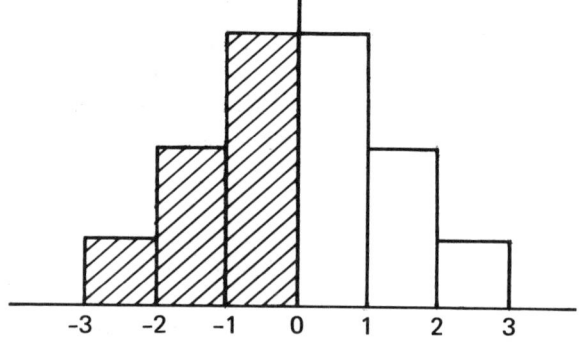

Probabilility Density Functions

We have already noted the trade-off between the number of intervals in a histogram and the accuracy of the representation. Relatively few intervals may yield overly gross representations, since all values within a given histogram interval are assumed to have the same likelihood of occurrence. On the other hand, increasing the number of intervals, and thereby narrowing the interval widths, increases the work involved in assessing probabilities and depicting results.

Fortunately, any given histogram will approach a limiting form as the interval widths are narrowed. The limiting form is called a *probability density function* (PDF), or simply a probability distribution. Most PDF's can be concisely described by one or two mathematical equations. These statements are illustrated in Figure 3-5, which shows two different ways of depicting information about the uncertain quantity "total U.S. market for new cars in 1978." The second histogram in Figure 3-5 conveys more information than the first. A close look at the 5- to 7-million car interval discloses the reason. Narrowing the interval widths in histogram 2 shows that values around 7 million are more likely than those around 5 million. Histogram 1 obscures that fact.

Figure 3-5. Two of the many ways of constructing a histogram for the same uncertain quantity.

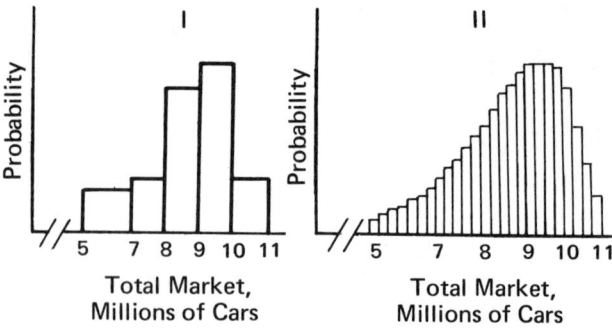

Thus we prefer, when possible, to work with very narrow intervals. To obviate the labor involved, we use the *envelope* of the histogram, the PDF, as shown in Figure 3-6, for the total new car market example. As is true of the histogram, the area under a PDF denotes probability. The height of the curve may be interpreted as relative likelihood.

Figure 3-6. An illustrative probability density function.

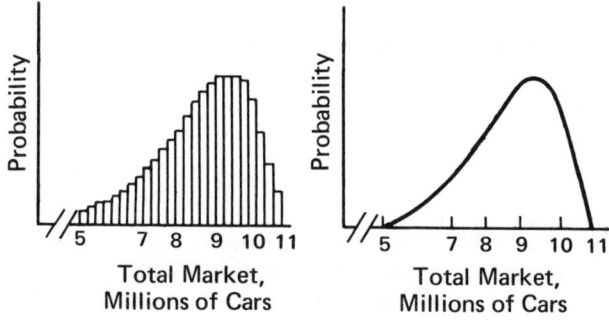

A third graphical display is the *cumulative distribution function* (CDF). It is derived from an associated histogram or PDF, and it shows the same information as the other displays but in a different way. Figure 3-7 is an illustration. The CDF is a plot of *cumulative* probability versus the possible values of the uncertain quantity, the total market. The cumulative probability of a specified value of total market is the probability that actual total market will be less than or equal to that value. For example, the CDF of Figure 3-7 shows that the probability of a total market of less than or equal to 10 million cars is 0.85. That value, 0.85, is also the area under the PDF, Figure 3-6, for total market between the lower limit (5 million) and 10 million. Thus the CDF shows basically the same information as the PDF, but in a little different presentation.

Figure 3-7. Cumulative distribution function for the total U.S. market for new cars in 1978.

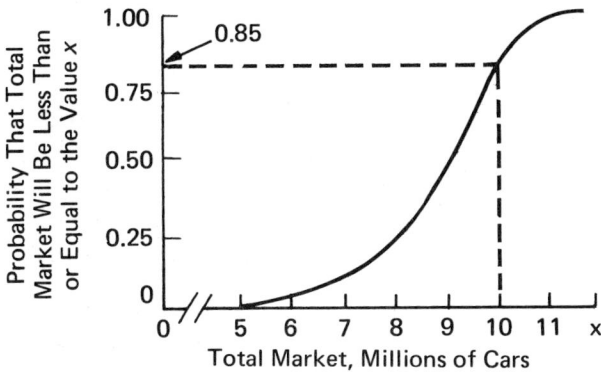

CDF's have different shapes for different uncertain quantities, but all CDF's have the following common features:

1. The vertical value (probability) always increases or remains constant as the value on the horizontal axis increases.
2. The probability that the uncertain quantity will be less than its lowest possible value is always zero.
3. The probability that the uncertain quantity will be less than its largest possible quantity is always 1 (a certainty).

A manifestation of the three preceding observations is that most CDF's have an "S shape."

Summary Statistics

There are many summary statistics that convey various kinds of information about graphical displays. We are interested in three of them: the *percentile*, the *expected value*, and the *variance* of an uncertain quantity.

The *p*th *percentile* of a probability distribution is the number that is larger than or equal to *p* percent of the possible values of the uncertain quantity that is represented by the distribution. To illustrate, the 15th percentile of the distribution of the total 1978 new car market (Figure 3-8) is 7 million cars, since 15 percent of the distribution lies below 7 million. Percentile values are used extensively in *sensitivity analysis,* a procedure that is described in Chapter 6.

Figure 3-8. Illustrating a percentile value.

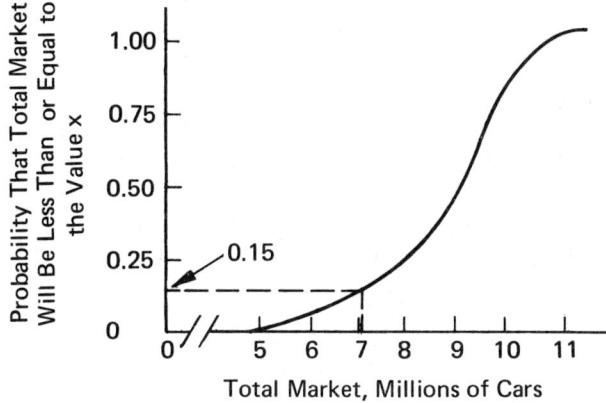

A second summary statistic is *expected value* of an uncertain quantity, which is the *average value* we would expect in the long run. To cite an instance, your *expected return on investment* from playing roulette might be minus 5 percent, which means that, on the average, you would lose 5 percent of your bet. Of course, any *one* bet might have only two outcomes: double your money or lose it all. However, in the absence of better information—or coupled with better information—the expected or average value is an extremely useful piece of information, even for one-time events.

In Chapter 5, we will have occasion to compute some expected values. When the number of possible values of an uncertainty quantity is small, the computation is a simple matter; Table 3-2 illustrates the method. Suppose, as shown in Table 3-2, that the economic life of a proposed investment has three possible values: 5, 10, and 15 years. The likelihood of occurrence of those values is felt to be 0.70, 0.20, and 0.10, respectively. Then the expected economic life is the *weighted* average of all possible values of economic life, whereas the weight assigned to a particular value is its probability of occurrence.

Table 3-2. An illustrative expected value computation.

Economic Life (Years)	Probability of Occurrence
5	0.80
10	0.20
15	0.10

Expected economic life = 0.80(5) + 0.20(10) + 0.10(15)
　　　　　　　　　　　= 4.0 + 2.0 + 1.5
　　　　　　　　　　　= 7.5 years

A third statistic of interest in risk analysis is the *variance* of an uncertain quantity. Variance is a measure of the *dispersion* of possible values about the expected value, and it is thus a measure of *uncertainty*. Qualitatively speaking, the larger the variance, the greater the uncertainty surrounding a quantity. Figure 3-9 shows probability density functions for two uncertain quantities that have identical expected values but different variances. Sometimes the *standard deviation* is used as a measure of dispersion or uncertainty. The standard deviation of an uncertain quantity is merely the square root of its variance.

Figure 3-9. Probability density functions for two uncertain quantities with identical expected values and different variances.

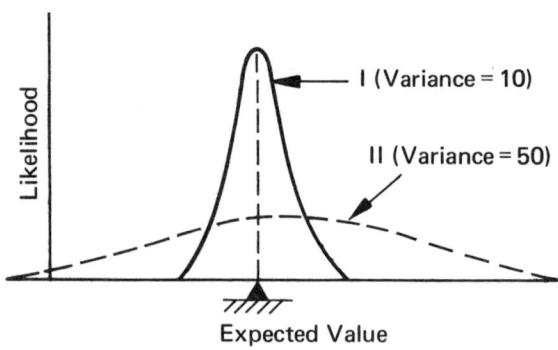

Histogram or Probability Density Function

Often, in risk analysis, we are fortunate in being able to deal with PDF's directly. An example is the determination of so-called three-point estimates for quantities of interest, wherein a *triangular* or other PDF is fitted to an individual's pessimistic, most likely, and optimistic estimates. Thus, if asked to estimate the economic life of a proposed investment, an individual might respond as follows:

Pessimistic value = 7 years
Most likely value = 10 years
Optimistic value = 20 years

One possible synthesized probability density function for those data is shown in Figure 3-10.

Generally, however, the use of PDF's is restricted to the input side of risk analysis. The output of a risk analysis is almost always a histogram. That fact derives largely from the process used to solve mathematical models in which the variables are *random*. The process, called *simulation*, is detailed in the following section.

Figure 3-10. An illustrative subjective probability density function.

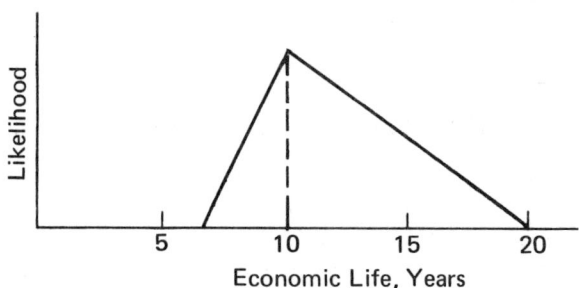

Simulation

Simulation is defined as the appearance without the reality. Striking examples of simulation were the depictions of manned lunar expeditions on television during the portions of the flight that were without live TV coverage.

Dynamic analysis specialists interested in the performance of automobile suspension systems frequently employ analog methods to simulate the response of those systems to programmed inputs. Of direct concern here, however, is a third type of simulation: the type used to *solve* certain kinds of mathematical models. Some of those mathematical simulations are *deterministic*, in that the values of all the variables in the mathematical model are assumed to be known with certainty. Others are *stochastic* or probabilistic, which simply means that the variables in the model are uncertain quantities. The use of simulation to solve stochastic mathematical models is often termed Monte Carlo simulation. or digital simulation, since the method generally requires the use of a digital computer.

The role of simulation in risk analysis is next illustrated. The following simple equation is a mathematical model that relates revenues from a new market investment to certain variables. We assume that the numerical values of the variables are known with certainty. In this instance, the solution of the equation is trivial; it entails merely the multiplication of three numbers.

The *mathematical model* is

$$R = SOM(TM)(P)$$

where

R = gross revenue in year x, dollars
SOM = share of market in year x, fraction
TM = total market in year x, units
P = unit selling price, dollars

The *model inputs* are

SOM = 0.40
TM = 100,000 units
P = $3 per unit

The *model solution* is

R = 0.40 (100,000) ($3) = $120,000

Now consider the same mathematical equation, but suppose that the variables SOM, TM, and P are uncertain quantities. In that case, their respective numerical values are PDF's (or histograms) rather than known amounts. Figure 3-11 illustrates the difficulty encountered: it is not so easy to solve the stochastic model.

Here is where simulation comes in. Simulation methods are extremely valuable in solving problems similar to, and including, the one pictured in Figure 3-11. Simulation is a computer-based, approximate-solution method. The inputs to the mathematical model may be histograms or PDF's; the outputs are generally in histogram form. Other solution methods exist, but they are generally less versatile and less powerful than simulation.

Figure 3-11. The mathematical model R = SOM(TM)(P), the variables in which are random.

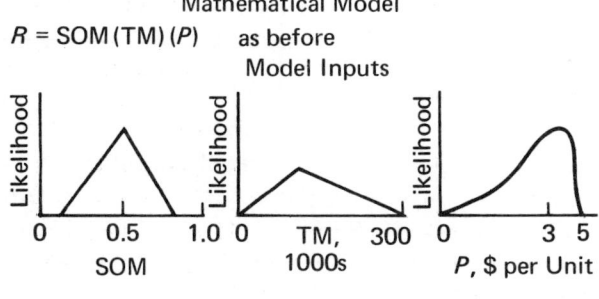

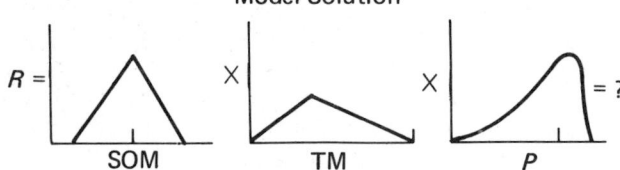

An Overview of the Simulation Process

One important point must be clarified before the use of simulation in financial risk analysis can be discussed in a meaningful way. It concerns the definition of the term "probability."

We stated earlier that the subjective definition of probability plays a major role in financial risk analysis. Furthermore, we noted that events amenable to treatment by using subjective probability need not be repeatable; they may be one-time events. In fact, most of the events of interest in financial risk analysis cannot be repeated. However, in applying simulation methods in risk analysis, we must imagine that, conceptually, all events of interest *can* be repeated an indefinite number of times. That the conceptualization is artificial has no effect on the validity of results for nonrepeatable events. It is merely a necessary mental step in understanding the process of simulation.

If events are viewed as being repeatable, then the relative frequency definition of probability can be applied in determining the outputs of financial risk analyses. Recall from preceding discussions that probability estimates are ratios or relative frequencies in the long run.

Let us first illustrate the simulation process, which entails the concept of repeated trials. Numerical values for each of the variables in the model are simulated in each trial, and the model is solved in each trial as though it were deterministic. The frequency of occurrence of solution values then forms the basis for determining output probability estimates.

Table 3-3 shows 10 trials of a simulation for the revenue model discussed previously. On each trial, values for share of market, total market, and price are simulated

Table 3-3. Ten trials for the revenue model simulation.

Mathematical Model

R = SOM(TM)(P)   as before

Model Inputs

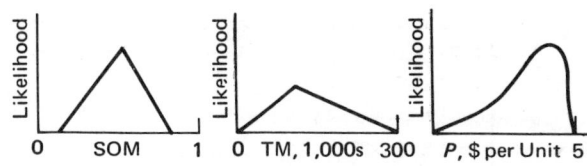

Simulation Results

Trial Number	Simulated Values			Resultant Revenue R
	SOM	TM	P	
1	0.54	90,000	$2.50	$121,500
2	0.42	45,000	2.70	51,030
3	0.46	150,000	2.20	151,800
4	0.28	105,000	4.30	126,420
5	0.65	110,000	3.10	221,650
6	0.45	220,000	3.50	346,500
7	0.50	80,000	4.00	160,000
8	0.32	98,000	1.90	59,580
9	0.25	250,000	3.00	187,500
10	0.40	120,000	3.30	158,400

from their respective probability distributions, and the model is solved by multiplying the resulting three values together. The result of the simulation is therefore 10 values for revenue *R*.

Table 3-4. Categorization of the revenue simulation results (ten trials).

Revenue Interval ($000)	Number of Trials in Which Revenue Was in Interval	Estimated Probability That Revenue Will Be in Interval
0–100	2	0.20
100–200	6	0.60
200–300	2	0.20
300–400	0	0.00
400–1,000	0	0.00
Total	10	1.00

The 10 values are displayed in histogram form by first defining class intervals for the histogram, as shown in Table 3-4. (Again, the definition of interval limits was somewhat arbitrary.) As the table shows, simulated revenue was between 0 and 100,000 on 20 percent of the trials, between $100,001 and $200,000 on 60 percent of the trials, and so forth. The data are displayed in histogram format in Figure 3-12. Note that the graph is not particularly meaningful in that probability estimates were derived from relative frequency for a mere 10 trials.

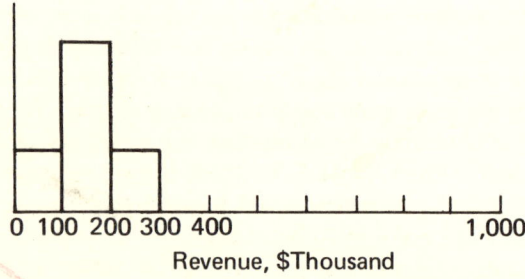

Figure 3-12. Histogram of results of revenue model simulation (ten trials).

Thus there are two interrelated factors that necessitate a large number of trials (usually hundreds) in simulation:

1. There must be a large number of results in a given interval before we can have confidence in the estimated probability for that interval.
2. The intervals must be narrow and thus numerous if an accurate picture of the true underlying probability density function is to result.

In a nutshell, then, the results of a simulation may be misleading if too few trials are simulated. Objective tests for determining the optimal number of trials to run can be found in most statistics textbooks.

Sampling from Probability Functions

The methods of simulating numbers from probability density functions are collectively termed *random number generation.* A nontechnical description of random number generation was given in Chapter 1. What follows is a slightly more technical treatment of the process.

Suppose that we were to simulate or sample numbers from the PDF shown in Figure 3-13. The function is a *uniform* distribution: all values between 0 and 1 are equally likely to occur, and all other values are impossible. Numbers can be "sampled" from the uniform distribution by repeatedly spinning a pointer on a wheel whose circumference is numbered from 0 to 1. Each stopping position of the pointer will be a sampled number. The property of the numbers will be that, *in the long run,* all numbers between 0 and 1 will appear with equal frequency, as indicated by the PDF.

Figure 3-13. A uniform probability density function.

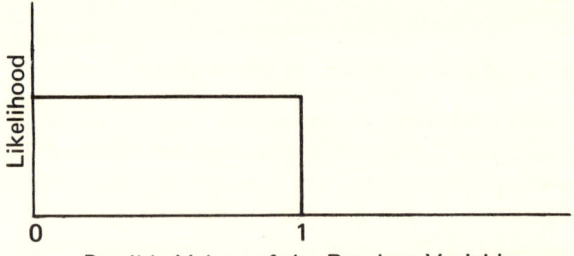

Today, in practice, uniform random numbers (that is, random numbers from the uniform distribution shown in Figure 3-13) are simulated by using mathematical models called pseudo random number generators. Random numbers from other distributions, such as the triangular distribution, are generated by using those uniform random numbers. That is exemplified by the graphical *probability integral transformation* method next discussed.

Suppose that we want to simulate, or sample, a number from the probability distribution for the uncertain quantity "total market." The cumulative distribution function for total market is shown in Figure 3-14. The sampling procedure is as follows:

1. Generate a uniform random number by using the mathematical methods described here. Suppose that the number is 0.63.
2. Locate the value 0.63 on the vertical axis of the CDF and draw a horizontal line from that point to the "east" to the CDF curve itself.

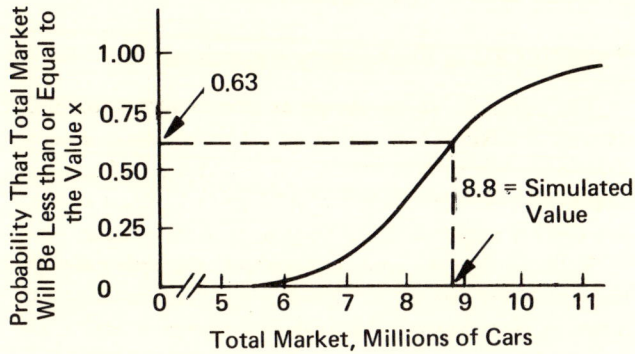

Figure 3-14. An illustration of the probability integral transformation method.

3. Make a 90-degree turn to the "south" with your pencil and continue the now-vertical line to the horizontal axis of the CDF.

4. The point of intersection of the vertical line that you drew with the horizontal axis is the simulated value from the distribution of total market. In Figure 3-14 that value is 8.8 million.

There are many other ways to simulate values from probability distributions. Most of them are mathematical and make the use of a computer desirable.

An Application of the Mathematical Tools

Before we move on to Chapter 4, it will be useful to consider one illustration that ties together the three tools: modeling, probability, and simulation. Moreover, the particular example given here illustrates some of the drawbacks of decision making under assumed certainty. The advantages of the risk analysis approach will be apparent in the example, which follows.

Two competitive proposals are being evaluated for the new Arnold tank. Analysis of technical characteristics has indicated that the designs are of equivalent quality, so the decision will be made on the basis of system acquisition cost.

The production costs for tanks follow learning curves similar to those developed in the aircraft industry. That is, the unit cost of the Nth item is given by

$$Y_N = AN^B$$

where Y_N = unit cost of Nth production item
 A = cost of first item
 B = learning curve exponent

We are interested in the total production cost (TC), which is the sum of the unit costs of the items. That is,

$$TC = \sum_{i=1}^{N} Y_i$$

It can be shown that this total cost is approximately equal to

$$TC = \frac{AN^{(B+1)}}{B+1}$$

Two contractors have submitted estimates for each of these factors, Table 3-5. The initial estimate of the quantity required is 150 units. On that basis the calculated acquisition costs (excluding contractor profits) are as given in Table 3-6. The analysis suggests that design 2 is to be preferred. The input cost factors are subject to some uncertainty, however, which may alter our conclusions. Further discussions with the contractors have yielded the estimates of the uncertainty of those cost factors given in Table 3-7.

Table 3-5.

Design	Initial Cost ($)	Learning Percent	Parameter B
1	1,200,000	84	−0.2519
2	900,000	88	−0.1844

Table 3-6.

Design	Production Cost ($)	Profit at 10%	Total Cost ($)
1	68,101,250	6,810,000	74,911,250
2	65,703,000	6,570,000	72,273,000

Risk analysis methodologies are valuable here, in that they will demonstrate forcefully that selecting design 2 on the basis of most likely estimates leads to a decision that is apt to be quite costly to the government. We can see that intuitively by examining the variability of the estimates. From Table 3-7, which shows estimates of variability of parameters A and B in the total cost equation, we can make two observations. First, the range of estimates for design 2 is greater than for design 1. Second, the most likely estimate for design 2 is nearer the optimistic value than is the corresponding estimate for design 1.

Figure 3-15 shows the results of 9,000 simulations for design 1. The distribution of total system cost is roughly symmetrical about the mean, $74.99 million, and ranges from about $62 to $89 million. The distribution of total system cost for design 2 is quite broad; the mean is $83.78 million and the range is from about $60 million to as high as $120 million. For that case the mean, $83.78 million, is much higher than that calculated from

Table 3-7.

Design	Parameter	Optimistic Value	Likely Value	Pessimistic Value
1	Cost of first item ($)	1,100,000	1,200,000	1,300,000
	Learning percent	82	84	86
	Parameter B	−0.2863	−0.2519	−0.2175
2	Cost of first item ($)	800,000	900,000	1,200,000
	Learning percent	86	88	94
	Parameter B	−0.2176	−0.1844	−0.0892

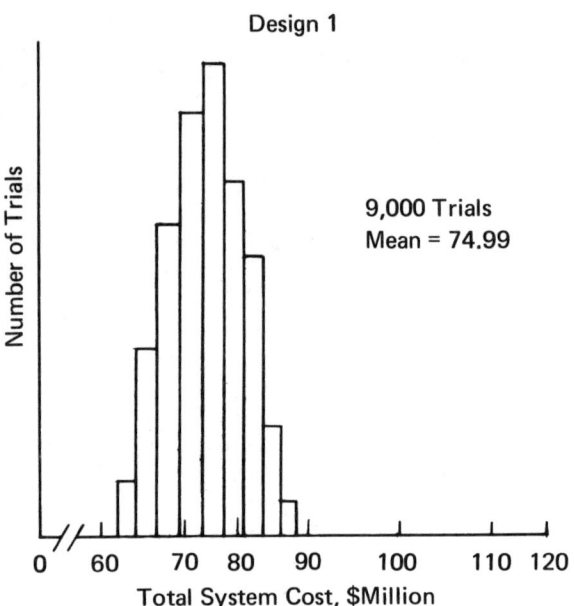

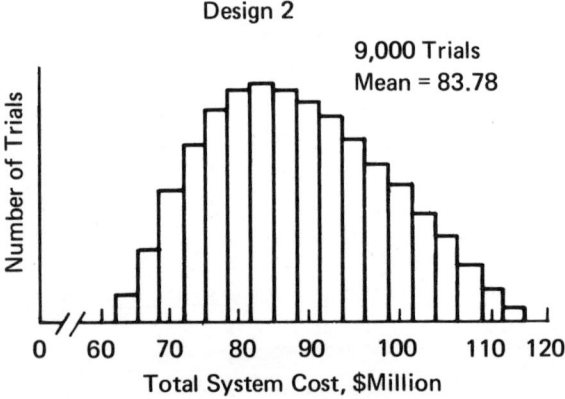

Figure 3-15. Results of simulation for Arnold tank designs 1 and 2.

most likely estimate, $72.27 million. Thus, we are led to select design 1 on the basis of lower average cost and lower variability.

Summary

Risk analysis is based on the use of probabilistic mathematical models and Monte Carlo simulation for solving those models. A mathematical model is merely an equation that relates some uncertain quantity of interest to a number of variables. The primary use of models in risk analysis is to improve predictive accuracy.

Probability theory can be used to great advantage to manipulate and display all of the information concerning random variables that exists. Random variables are quantities that have many possible values and whose ultimate exact value cannot be predicted with absolute certainty.

Two definitions of probability are in common use. According to the first one, the probability of occurrence of an event is the relative frequency of occurrence of that event in the long run. Relative frequency implies repeatability of the event.

According to the subjective definition, on the other hand, probability is merely quantified judgment. In that sense, the event of interest need not be repeatable.

The portrayal of probabilistic information entails the use of graphical displays (probability density function, cumulative distribution function) and summary statistics (expected value, mode, median, variance, and standard deviation).

Monte Carlo simulation is the most popular and most powerful method available for solving probabilistic mathematical models.

Wisdom is opinion with charisma.

N.C. Dalkey
The Delphi Method: An Experimental Study of Group Opinion

4
Obtaining Inputs to a Risk Analysis

Preceding chapters in this briefing have explored some of the technical aspects of a risk analysis, principally from the point of view of processing information inputs in order to select, derive, and calculate probabilistic measures of investment worth. In this chapter we turn our attention to the processes of obtaining the inputs to the risk analysis. The importance of the task is obvious, because the quality of the outputs is directly related to the quality of the inputs. (Recall the famous adage GIGO, or garbage in, garbage out.) Despite that importance, there is an unfortunate tendency among practitioners to focus on the technically interesting aspects of an analysis rather than the "less elegant" (and more frustrating!) tasks required for an effective analysis.

It has been our experience that effort expended in gathering inputs is well worthwhile from the point of view not only of obtaining valid inputs to the analysis under consideration but, equally important, of providing insight that is valuable in interpreting the outputs of an analysis. Also, the process of generating inputs frequently leads to a better definition of existing alternatives and the basis for defining additional ones. What are the inputs required for a risk analysis? Broadly speaking, they are of three basic types.

Alternatives and Policies

Input elements of the first type relate to management policy or alternative strategies. As an example, management may wish to establish a policy that investments must earn at least x percent ROI, or it may wish to set limits on the commitment of resources to one area or segment of business. The policies are translated either into constraints in the risk analysis evaluation (as the resource limitation would be) or into numerical values for certain evaluation parameters (such as the use of y percent as a cost of capital in the discount rate). It is frequently valuable to vary policies systematically and note the impact of the changes on calculated measures of worth. In that way the *opportunity cost* of the policies can be expressed and the policies can be reexamined in an economic framework.

Included also in this first class of inputs is the identification of investment and strategy alternatives. As an example, in the introduction of a new product, several alternative investment strategies can be envisaged. One strategy might be to test-market the product on a regional basis and, if "sufficient" market develops, introduce the product nationally. Variants might include in-house versus out-of-house production (basically the substitution of fixed for variable costs) during regional introduction. An alternative strategy might involve immediate national introduction with either production alternative.

Accounting Conventions

The second class of inputs to risk analysis includes the specification of the measures of investment worth to be employed in the analysis, depreciation methods and lifetimes, and the tax status of the proposed alternatives (for example, whether the new venture will result in the creation of a subsidiary and the applicability and amount of investment tax credits). In short, these inputs are derived from measures of worth and the relations on which calculation of those measures from revenues, costs, and investments is based.

Numerical Inputs

Inputs of the third class are numerical estimates of market size, share of market, and fixed and variable costs of manufacturing and distribution, sales, advertising and promotion, and so on. Frequently the numerical inputs will involve parameters that are related to the variables identified by mathematical models rather than those inputs directly. Thus, instead of describing the direct variable manufacturing cost per unit over all time periods in the planning horizon, we may have a mathematical model that relates that cost per unit to an initial cost per unit and cumulative production. An example of such a model is the learning curve that has been found useful in the analysis of airframe costs. Numerical inputs are related to alternatives and policies, the first class of inputs.

The three kinds of input are, of course, required even for a conventional analysis. The special character of the inputs when used in a risk analysis is that uncertainty is explicitly considered. That is particularly true of numerical inputs. Ideally, a given input factor is specified as a probability distribution that reflects the best guesstimates of the uncertainty inherent in the variable. The sources of that information and the appropriate techniques for analysis are legion. Broadly speaking, we can classify the inputs as hard estimates, which are derived from either empirical data or verified models, and soft estimates. Much less is known of soft estimates than of hard ones, usually because of limited past data, a perception that past data cannot be extrapolated, or an absence of validated relationships to be used for estimation. Hard estimates might, for example, be those for the manufacturing costs of a chemical process based upon known technology and raw material costs, possibly supplemented by direct manufacturing experience. In contrast, if the process involves novel technology or employs raw materials that have undergone or are expected to undergo considerable price fluctuation (for example, certain natural chemicals as opposed to synthetics), then estimates are likely to be much softer. There is no precise line between hard and soft estimates; instead there is a continuum of possibilities. Nonetheless, the distinction is convenient and useful for exploring techniques and obtaining and analyzing the inputs.

Much has been written on techniques that employ hard data, and so those techniques will not be discussed here; see books by Brown (3), Johnston (17), Hadley (12), and Box and Jenkins (2), and a survey article by Chambers et al. (5). Instead, our focus will be on less well known and explored techniques that are more qualitative in nature and are appropriate for soft data.

Off-the-Cuff Estimates

So-called off-the-cuff (OTC) estimates by informed staff or subject area experts are one source of soft inputs. Despite the rather casual title, the method can be made quite systematic by categorically defining assumptions and limitations and performing numerous consistency checks. An excellent example of the way an OTC estimate can be obtained is furnished by Howard Raiffa (22) in the form of a hypothetical dialogue between an analyst and his client. In this case the quantity to be estimated is the proportion of medical doctors who consume more scotch than bourbon. This dialogue is presented in its entirety:[1]

> **Analyst.** I should like to show you how you can obtain a judgmental probability distribution for some unknown proportion p. I want to choose a context that is sufficiently meaningful to you, because *I* want to probe into *your* judgments rather than into someone else's. Let's consider the population of medical doctors in the U.S. who are nonteetotalers. Now suppose we let p be the proportion of these imbibers who consumed more scotch than bourbon in the past year. Incidentally, do you know much about the drinking pattern of doctors?
>
> **Subject.** Not much. The usual, I suppose. I know three or four doctors personally, but I imagine doctors are not much different from lawyers or dentists or engineers. The trouble is that I would not know how to answer your question for any of those groups. I don't have the foggiest notion what p is.

---

[1] Reproduced with the kind permission of Addison-Wesley Corporation.

Analyst. Good. I wanted to take just such an example.

Subject. I suppose you want me to give a best guess at p. I don't know if I could even do that.

Analyst. No, I don't want you to do that. In fact, I don't think it's very meaningful to talk about a 'best' guess. Best for what? Let me start off with some warming-up questions. Do you think it's more likely that p is less than .10 or above .10?

Subject. That's easy! Above.

Analyst. Is it more likely that p is above .90 or below?

Subject. Below.

Analyst. Those were easy. See, you do know something about p. Now I want you to think hard about the next one. Give me a value such that it would be extremely hard for you to make up your mind to choose above it or below it. In other words, I want you to give me a value such that you will think it equally likely that p falls below or above it.

Subject. (After some thought.) I would say .60. But, boy, am I vague about this. I *think* more doctors prefer scotch. You know, the upwardly mobile group and all that sort of thing.

Analyst. Don't fret about this too much; if you want to change your mind later on, that's all right with me. You have now told me that you think it is equally likely that p is less than .60 or more than .60.

Subject. That's right. But don't ask me to define what 'equally likely' means.

Analyst. By 'equally likely' in this context I mean that you are indifferent between receiving a very desirable prize conditional on p being below .60 and receiving this identical prize conditional on p being above .60. Or, more dramatically, if your life depended on it, you would just as soon opt for $p \leq .60$ as $p \geq .60$. Are you with me?

Subject. So far, so good.

Analyst. Essentially you have now told me, *and* yourself, that .60 divides the interval from zero to 1.0 into two judgmentally equally likely parts. Now I am going to ask you to repeat this process of judgmentally subdividing different intervals into two equally likely parts. For example, do you think it is more likely that p is less than .20 or is between .20 and .60?

Subject. Between .20 and .60.

Analyst. Between zero and .58 or between .58 and .60?

Subject. Between zero and .58.

Analyst. All right, now give me a number such that you think it is judgmentally equally likely that p is between zero and that number or between that number and .60.

Subject. What happens if p is greater than .60?

Analyst. As things stand now, you lose. Look, if you tell me the number is p^*, then this means that you think your chances of winning the prize are just as good if you choose the interval zero to p^* as they are if you choose the interval p^* to .60. If p is greater than .60, you would not get the prize no matter which side of p^* you choose because p would not be in either interval.

Subject. All right, let's see. I'll say that .50 divides the interval zero to .60 into two equally likely parts.

Analyst. Once you had given me the number .60, would it have been easier for you if I had posed my last request this way: 'Look, suppose I tell you that p is less than .60. Knowing this, how would you divide the interval zero to .60 into two equally likely parts?

Subject. Are these the same questions?

Analyst. I think so. Think about it.

Subject. I suppose they are the same. The second way seems easier, but second ways always seem easier to me.

Analyst. Let's go on. Suppose I tell you that p is greater than .60. Then how would you divide the interval .60 to 1.00 into two equally likely parts?

Subject. Hmmm—.70. From .60 to .70 is just as likely as above .70. But I really feel uncomfortable about the .50 and .70 because the .60 is so shaky I feel I'm building on a sponge. I hope you realize these numbers are mighty shaky.

Analyst. I hope you realize that I realize that. You are doing fine. You have now given me three numbers, .60, .50, and .70. Let me draw an interval from zero to 1.00 and place these points on it:

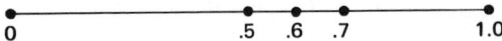

Now you have told me that so far as you are concerned, you believe it is just as likely that p lies in any one of the four intervals [0 to .50], [.50 to .60], [.60 to .70], and [.70 to 1.00].

Subject. I guess I said that.

Analyst. Now I am just checking up. I don't want to catch you and it certainly is not my intention to embarrass you, but it is important to look at these things from many different angles. For example, would you rather bet that *p* lies in the interval [.50 to .70], or outside this interval?

Subject. I think I would bet that it lies inside the interval. But now I'm being inconsistent, am I not?

Analyst. Yes, you are, but almost everyone else is too. I want you to think about it more. It will help if you try consciously to be consistent.

Subject. Well, I don't want to change the .60. I feel shakiest about the .70. I suppose I'd be willing to live with .68. So far as I'm concerned, it's a 50–50 bet that *p* lies in the interval [.50 to .68].

Analyst. Would you be willing to say that it is equally likely that *p* lies in the interval [.60 to .68] as in the interval [.68 to 1.00]?

Subject. All right, I'll go along with this. But if we did it all over again and if I erased this conversation from my memory, I can imagine that instead of ending up with the numbers .50, .60, and .68, I could have ended up with numbers like .52, .64, and .74.

Analyst. Well, these are in the same ballpark. Could you imagine ending up with numbers like .20, .40, and .55?

Subject. No. Not really. But what would you do if I said "Yes"?

Analyst. I would push you further and use some averaging process that would pull the three numbers you have given me further apart. But let's go on. I'll refer to the number .60 as your judgmental .50-fractile, the number .50 as your judgmental .25-fractile, and the number .68 as your judgmental .75-fractile.

Aside to the reader. Symbolically I shall write this as

$$p_{.25} = .50, \quad p_{.50} = .60, \quad p_{.75} = .68.$$

A few more numbers will help me. How would you divide the interval [0 to .50] into two equally likely parts?

Subject. .42.

Analyst. *Aside.* This means $p_{.125} = .42$.
Now divide the interval [.00 to .42].

Subject. You are pushing me pretty far.

Analyst. Well, suppose I told you that *p* is less than .42. Would you rather bet on [.00 to .21] or on [.21 to .42]?

Subject. On the latter, of course. All right, use .36.

Analyst. *Aside.* This means $p_{.0625} = .36$.
Now let's pass quickly to the high end. Divide [.68 to 1.00].

Subject. Use .75.

Analyst. *Aside.* This means $p_{.875} = .75$.
All right, divide [.75 to 1.00].

Subject. Use .80.

Analyst. *Aside.* This means $p_{.9375} = .80$.
Let's summarize your judgmental responses in a table:

Proportion p of Medical Doctors Who Prefer Scotch to Bourbon	Guesstimated Probability That Actual Proportion Is Less Than p
0.36	0.0625
0.42	0.1250
0.50	0.2500
0.60	0.5000
0.68	0.7500
0.75	0.8750
0.80	0.9325

The table provides several points on the judgmentally determined cumulative distribution function, and Figure 4-1 is a plot of that CDF. The analyst might attempt to fit a mathematical form to the empirical CDF or, alternatively, use the table itself as an input to the analysis program. The important concept for the reader to glean from the preceding example is the systematic *method* that

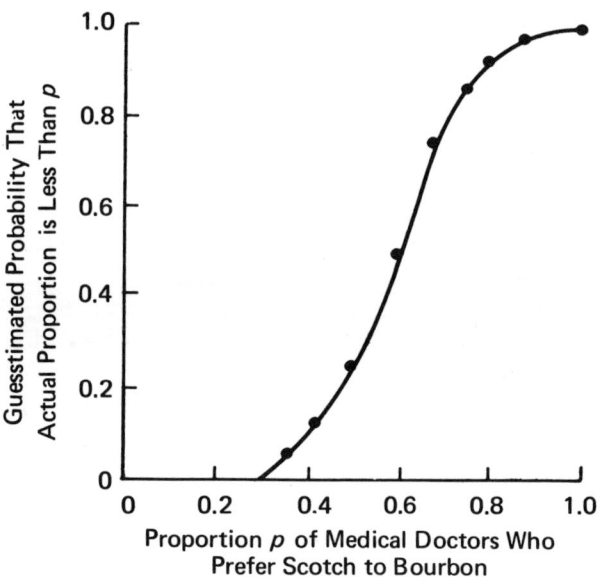

Figure 4-1. Off-the-cuff subjective probability distribution.

may be employed to assess the subjective probability distribution, rather than the use of the method to determine the particular issue in question. In fact, many alternative techniques might be employed to that end.

At this point some brief comments regarding the ease with which subjective probability distributions can be elicited and the reliability of the answers so obtained are in order. Some practitioners hold that derivation of probabilistic information is relatively difficult because the mind has limited information-handling capabilities. They argue that the elimination of uncertainty effects a material simplification of the process of estimation. For an exposition of that view see Morris.(20) Although the information-handling factor is no doubt operative, many analysts have found that the determination of a probability distribution is little more difficult than obtaining point estimates for investment variables. Moreover, the process is felt to be less subject to factors that systematically bias point estimates. David Hertz reflects the experience of McKinsey and Company, Inc. in stating (16):

> It has been our experience that for major capital proposals managements usually make a significant investment in time and funds to pinpoint information about each of the relevant factors. An objective analysis of the values to be assigned to each can, with little additional effort, yield a subjective probability distribution.

That experience has been shared by Norman C. Dalkey (6) of The Rand Corporation in studying the properties of the Delphi method; he found that estimates of selected percentiles of distribution were made quite naturally by his subjects: "Somewhat to our surprise, the subjects had no difficulty in making these presumably more complex estimates." Donald H. Woods (25), writing in the *Harvard Business Review,* argues that estimates obtained in this manner are less likely to reflect bias than single-point estimates.

These latter views are entirely in accord with our own experience in conducting risk analysis for both government and commercial clients. Most individuals have little or no difficulty in responding to carefully phrased questions. Moreover, they are inherently more comfortable in couching their answers in a probabilistic framework, which more accurately reflects their state of knowledge than any single-point estimate could.

OTC estimates by individuals will no doubt be the way to obtain many of the inputs necessary for a risk analysis. Certain data, however, will be of a critical nature; that is, project profitability is strongly dependent upon accurately estimating the ranges in which such numbers might fall. (The way in which those critical variables are identified, called sensitivity analysis, is discussed in Chapter 6.) For the critical variables, more elaborate procedures are warranted. We will discuss two of them, the consensus technique and the Delphi technique.

Consensus Methods

The old adage that two heads are better than one (generalized by N. C. Dalkey to n heads are better than one) provides the basis for techniques that seek to pool the judgment of several qualified sources. The basic rationale behind the procedure is that at least as much information is possessed by several sources or experts as by any one of them.

Consensus techniques operate generally as follows: Knowledgeable individuals—or experts if you prefer—are asked to provide information on critical parameters of interest. That information consists of numerical estimates together with whatever data exist to support those estimates. The material is presented and discussed openly in a series of group meetings in an attempt to arrive at a consensus. Between meetings, participants are free to rethink the problem, acquire additional supporting data, reanalyze their own or other participants' data, and revise their estimates. The process continues until a group consensus is reached or it is agreed that a consensus is impossible.

The procedure can be seen to have a number of drawbacks that are familiar to anyone who has ever served on a committee and also to psychologists who are interested in group behavior (Refs. 1, 18, 19). The main ones (after Dalkey) are influence of dominant individuals, semantic noise, and group pressure for conformity. That these factors are real is unquestionable; what is relevant is the *extent* to which they act to reduce the effectiveness of the group. A mounting body of evidence suggests that a consensus technique is little more (and possibly *less*) accurate than polling individuals (Refs. 4, 8, 10). One series of experiments conducted at The Rand Corporation indicated that the median of the off-the-cuff estimates of individuals prior to discussion was *more* accurate than the group consensus. The difficulties that are inherent in consensus techniques have prompted the development of other techniques for pooling information in an attempt to obviate the difficulties while retaining the n-heads advantage. The most prominent of the other techniques is one developed by Helmer and Dalkey at The Rand Corporation. It is termed the Delphi technique (Refs. 6, 8-10, 13-15).

The Delphi Technique

The Delphi technique incorporates three main features

to eliminate disadvantages of the consensus approach; they are anonymity, statistical summarization of group response, and controlled feedback. One way in which a Delphi exercise might be run is as follows: A questionnaire is sent to all participants of the panel of experts; it defines the variable to be estimated and also key assumptions or ground rules that the participants should take to be the givens of the problem. Each participant then formulates his estimate (either as a single point or, preferably, as a probability distribution). The participants are also asked to identify any other assumptions that underlie their analysis. The responses are then summarized statistically by the analyst who is conducting the exercise. Typically, the summarization includes the distribution of all results and a statement of where each respondent's estimate falls in relation to other estimates. Respondents are asked to rethink the problem and submit revised estimates if they think revision is appropriate.

In one variant of the Delphi procedure advocated by Helmer (15), respondents whose estimates are substantially different from the group median (higher than 75 percent or lower than 25 percent of the group's estimates) are asked to state briefly why they think the variable should be lower or higher than the majority put it. The reasons are then edited and resubmitted to the group together with the revised distribution of estimates, and that procedure is continued for another round or so. Usually the distribution of responses becomes less disperse and the group reaches a consensus, but sometimes opinions tend to polarize around two or more sets of values. Often, when opinions do polarize, the respondents differ not with regard to estimates given the identical assumptions, but rather with regard to *which assumptions* are justified. An illustration of how assumptions influence estimates is furnished in a somewhat different context by Woods (25):

> In one case involving the decision process for making gasoline station investments, a manager—call him Manager A—arbitrarily classified one potential site as a "captive station." (A captive station is one which the customer has to use if he needs gasoline, because there is no other station around. An example is the turnpike station.) The manager's forecast of gallon sales was based on this classification; the estimate would have been quite a bit lower if the station had not been considered a captive. In making his estimate, the manager compared the proposed site with an operative captive station he was familiar with.
>
> However, another decision maker—call him Manager B—in a similar organizational position in a comparable company decided that this same potential site was "noncaptive," and compared it directly to the site of a noncaptive station with which he was familiar. Hence his estimate was far more conservative than the first manager's—400,000 gallons annually, against 1,000,000. This variance in the estimates—250%—clearly appeared to be more than could be attributed to simple differences in judgment regarding a fairly routine problem.

In this example, the process of attempting to reach a consensus in estimation produced an important byproduct, namely, the identification of a critical assumption. Attention could then be focused on resolving the issue of whether or not the station is likely to be captive (expressed perhaps as a probability). Also, a number of subsidiary questions might be raised. For example, if the station is in fact captive, is it likely to remain so indefinitely (as it might if it were a turnpike station) or might competition arise? If so, when? The point is that the process of obtaining inputs, if carefully structured, can provide insight into the decision problem and, indeed, can enrich the model and analysis.

Another example of value arising from failure to achieve a consensus was the risk analysis of a research and development project for an improved armored vehicle launched bridge for the U.S. Army. Opinion that the effort could be successfully concluded within time and budget constraints polarized about two probabilities, one quite high and the other unacceptably low. Upon examination, it was found that there was a basic disagreement over the existence of a technology for high-strength welding of the new aluminum alloy that was to be used to fabricate the bridge. That brought to the surface a key technical uncertainty of the project and, moreover, suggested several useful alternatives. First, a feasibility study could be conducted to evaluate whether the material could be reliably welded. That study could be conducted for a small fraction of the cost of the development contract. A second alternative was that experience of the bidders in welding the material should be an important factor in proposal evaluation. Ultimately, both alternatives were adopted. Again, inquiry into the reasons for the failure of the estimating procedure to converge led to useful insights and improved alternatives.

Generally, the use of the Delphi procedure results in convergence rather than polarization, but convergence alone does not imply correctness. History is replete with occasions on which the consensus estimates of experts were manifestly wrong. Quinn (21) cites an interesting one:

> In the early 1950's savants estimated that only some 30 electronic computers would be needed to handle all the calculations then being made by

every bookkeeper, scientist, and technologist in the United States. This seeming lack of demand discouraged most potential manufacturers from entering the field. Only when actual use demonstrated that the computer made it possible to attack problems previously beyond imagination did the true nature of the market become apparent. In effect, the enormous new capacity to compute served to stimulate people to think of more complex problems requiring computation.

Moreover, the technique of asking respondents to justify extreme views (albeit anonymously) still creates certain artificial pressures for convergence, something that the Delphi procedure is designed to circumvent. The important practical question, however, is whether successive revision of estimates produces answers that are more *consistent* or answers that are more *accurate* in the sense of being closer to the true value. Also, we are concerned with whether the Delphi technique produces better estimates than other consensus procedures. At present there are no conclusive answers to these questions, but a number of studies have tended to verify two hypotheses:

1. Delphi procedures are likely to produce estimates of greater accuracy than comparable consensus approaches.
2. Answers tend to improve with iteration.

In one series of experiments conducted by Campbell (4), graduate students were asked to develop forecasts for some 16 economic indices. Both conventional methods (which permit face-to-face interaction) and Delphi methods were employed. The Delphi forecasts were more accurate on 13 of 16 indices. Moreover, when groups that had employed the Delphi method were allowed to have face-to-face interaction and come up with a consensus answer, the revised answers were less accurate in 75 to 80 percent of the cases. Experiments conducted by Dalkey (6) and also involving graduate students have suggested that Delphi estimates improve in successive rounds and are more accurate than consensus views. The results, while not conclusive (to what extent could we expect the same results with businessmen who are ego-involved with their problems?), are certainly encouraging. Our own experience in conducting risk analyses suggests that the Delphi technique is valuable.

Weighting Evidence

A question that arises from the use of several experts to arrive at an estimate is how to weigh views. If a consensus distribution is actually achieved by iteration, it can be used as an input, but when no clear consensus emerges, the analyst has the task of weighing alternative views or selecting a "best" view. The latter is a special form of weighting. Mathematically it is possible to define a simple weighting procedure in which each subjective probability distribution function is multiplied by appropriate weights. That is an approach recommended by Winkler.(24) If $F_1(x)$ and $F_2(x)$ denote the CDF's of experts 1 and 2, respectively, the pooled CDF is given by

$$F(x) = W_1 F_1(x) + W_2 F_2(x)$$

where W_1 and W_2 are the weights assigned to experts 1 and 2. It is necessary that W_1 and W_2 each be between 0 and 1 and that they sum to unity.

The Winkler procedure is illustrated by Figure 4-2, which shows the estimates of two experts of the first-year sales volume of a new industrial chemical. (Recall how you might determine each distribution.) If we choose to regard the experts as equally accurate in their estimates, then equal weights might be appropriate ($W_1 = 0.5$, $W_2 = 0.5$). The weighted distribution is also shown in Figure 4-2. The difficulty in employing the weighting scheme lies not in the mathematics, but in the choice of appropriate weights. The following suggestions on choosing weights have been advanced:

1. Equal weights are appropriate when there is no reason to prefer one expert's opinion over another's.

2. A weight might be chosen on the basis of the previous accuracy of the expert, as Schlaifer (23), among others, has suggested. The difficulty is that the analyst is not likely to have developed the data necessary as a basis for the weighting.

Figure 4-2. Weighted subjective probability distribution.

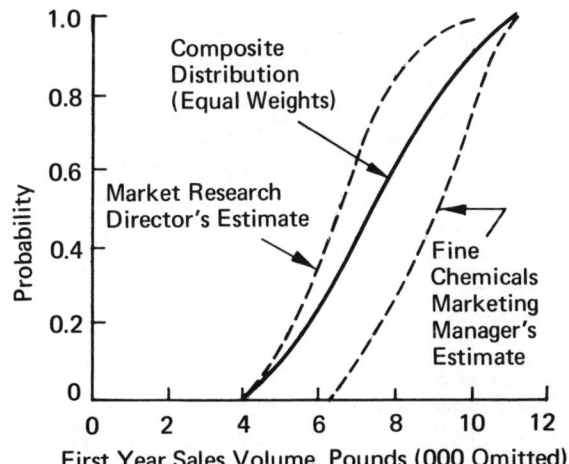

3. Each expert might be asked to rank himself, and the ranks might be normalized to form a set of weights. That proposition has not been fully explored, and the evidence that does exist is quite mixed. Helmer (14, 15) reports that self-ranking procedures (that lead to formation of elite subgroups) are useful and produce more accurate estimates. Other investigators have been less successful with self-ranking, as Dalkey (10) reports:

> One of the lowlights of our investigation so far is that we have not been able to find a criterion which enables the selection of such a subgroup. In particular, the use of a self-rating scale, either in terms of the relative confidence the subject has in his answers, or his relative performance vis-a-vis the group, has not offered a reliable way of singling out a superior subgroup.

In more recent work, Dalkey, Brown, and Cochran (11) report that a suitable combination of subgroup selection and controlled feedback can, under certain conditions, lead to improved accuracy in estimates. Our own view on the subject is that weighting should be done with great care if at all. It is unlikely that evidence is available for other than an arbitrary choice of weights. Our recommendation would be to try to find the reason for failure to achieve consensus rather than develop weighting schemes. If no such resolution emerges, we feel that more insight is to be gained by developing duplicate analyses using each input in turn rather than by weighting inputs.

Of course, the duplicate analysis is a feasible option only if the number of inputs about which significant disagreement exists is relatively small in number. Otherwise, the number of analyses grows prohibitively large, a phenomenon that D. Wilde calls the curse of dimensionality. To illustrate, if there are two significantly different viewpoints on each of N variables, the number of separate analyses required (if no weighting is employed) is 2^N. Table 4-1 will convince you of the impracticality of evaluating all possible combinations of views if N is greater than 2 or 3.

Table 4-1. Possible combinations of variables.

Number of Variables, N, About Which There Is a Substantive Disagreement	Number of Separate Analyses, 2^N, Required If No Weighting Scheme Is Employed
0	1
1	2
2	4
5	32
10	1,024
20	1,048,576
50	1,125,899,906,842,624

If there is substantial disagreement on several variables among experts, then some form of weighting procedure is essential if the analysis is to be tractable. In our experience, though, that situation has arisen relatively infrequently, and then most often because the investment or program under analysis was politically controversial: views on appropriate parameter values were intimately associated with views on the aggregate desirability of the project. In such cases the reliability of subjective probabilities is seriously open to question. It is probably worth the investment to try to obtain objective hard data rather than to debate points of view through manipulation of soft estimates.

Summary

Obtaining inputs to a risk analysis is an essential part of the total analysis. A valuable byproduct of the information-gathering process is increased insight into the problem itself, often in the form of highlighting critical factors and generating useful alternatives for analysis.

The first logical step in the determination of inputs is to obtain initial estimates that can be used to identify which input parameters are most important or critical, a process that is discussed in detail in Chapter 6. The sensitivity analysis can be used to allocate appropriate amounts of effort to the determination of each input factor.

Numerical input factors can be roughly grouped as hard and soft estimates. Hard estimates are best developed by using a well-established body of mathematical analysis. Soft or more subjective estimates require other techniques. Most soft inputs will be obtained from OTC estimates by informed staff members. The casual name "off-the-cuff estimates" should not suggest a casual process, however. Assumptions should be made explicit, and careful and systematic questioning should be employed.

For soft parameters that are highly critical to the problem at hand, more elaborate data-gathering procedures are warranted. Of these, the most famous and most useful is the Delphi method, which combines information from several experts in a way that best reflects collective judgment and is least affected by the bias factors inherent in confrontations.

Despite attempts to reach a consensus of expert judgment, substantive differences may occur. Provided that is true of only a few variables, separate analyses can best convey the impact of the differences to the decision maker. When a lack of consensus for more than a few parameters eventuates, some form of weighting procedure is indicated.

[It] is usually impossible to think through a decision that must be made now without at the same time thinking through some decision or decisions that may have to be made at some time in the future.

Robert Schlaifer
Analysis of Decisions Under Uncertainty

5
Interrelated Decisions Over Time

Decision making is the process of choosing from alternative courses of action. Often, the consequences of the choice will depend upon *events* that cannot be foreseen or cannot be predicted with absolute certainty. Moreover, as Schlaifer (5) has pointed out, there are future *decisions* or choices that directly affect the consequences of the immediate decision.

Ideally, the decision maker would consider all the future events and decisions that bear upon his immediate problem of choice. Unfortunately, man's information-processing capacity is limited, which renders simultaneous consideration of all relevant future factors impossible. Thus it is necessary to rely upon some efficient means of organizing and displaying all the factors that are relevant to the present choice.

The decision tree provides a systematic framework for organizing and portraying all the future events and actions that directly affect the results of the present decision. Decision trees are useful aids in *sequential decision problems,* that is, problems that involve a sequence of interrelated decisions over time. Useful references on this concept are found in Magee (3, 4), Hammond (1), and Schlaifer (5).

Decision Tree Structure

The main elements of a decision tree are *acts,* or *decisions,* and *chance events.* Acts, or decisions, are generally represented by squares and chance events by circles. Decision tree structure is most simply introduced by considering an illustrative single-stage decision problem, that is, one in which there are no future actions that directly affect the consequences of the immediate decision.

Imagine that you wish to decide whether or not to purchase a state lottery ticket. There are two courses of action available to you: either to purchase the ticket or not to purchase it. Two future chance events are relevant to your choice of a course of action. They are *win* and *lose,* and they follow, chronologically, a decision to purchase the lottery ticket.

Figure 5-1 shows the decision tree for our simple example. Notice that we have limited the problem by choosing a fixed and finite time horizon. Actions and events beyond that horizon are not considered. There is a basic trade-off between the realism afforded by longer time horizons (and hence "bushier" trees) and the computational tractability characteristic of small trees.

Figure 5-1. Decision tree for the lottery ticket example.

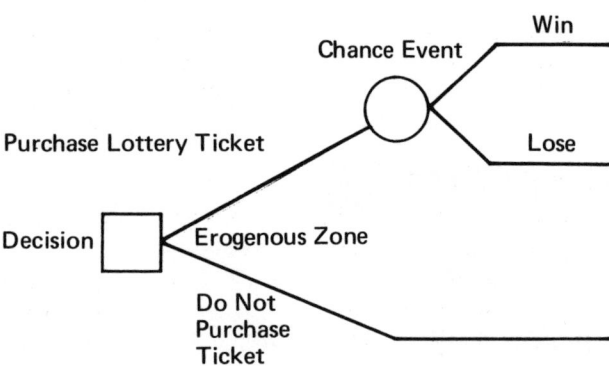

To make the decision tree a useful decision-making aid, it is necessary to choose a criterion or a set of criteria that will indicate preference for one action or the other. Many criteria are possible. Some are based on tangible measures of benefit, such as monetary gain; others depend upon intangible benefits, such as the prestige of the firm.

Since the decision tree, in common with other tools discussed in this briefing, is a quantitative tool, we shall concentrate on quantitative measurements of the consequences of decisions. Thus, let us assume that our objective in accepting or rejecting the opportunity to purchase the lottery ticket is to maximize our personal wealth. Suppose that the lottery ticket costs $2.50 and pays $100 to the holder of the winning ticket. Then the possible *payoffs* resulting from a decision to purchase the ticket are + $100 (win) and - $2.50 (lose). The payoff from the no-purchase decision is zero.

The problem of determining the action that maximizes wealth is not a trivial one, even in this simple problem, since the consequences of the decision are probabilistic. According to one widely used criterion, however, the preferred action is that which has the maximum *expected* payoff. Recall that expected value is the weighted average value that would occur if an action were repeated many times.

Since the weight applied to each possible value of payoff is the probability that the value occurs, it is necessary to provide probabilities for the events "win" and "lose" in the lottery illustration. Let p denote the probability of winning and $1-p$ denote the probability of losing. Then the complete decision tree is as shown in Figure 5-2. The expected payoff of a decision to purchase is $100p - \$2.50(1-p)$. If for a given probability p that expected value exceeds zero (the payoff of the no-purchase option), then according to our criterion, the lottery ticket should be purchased.

Figure 5-2. The complete decision tree for the lottery example.

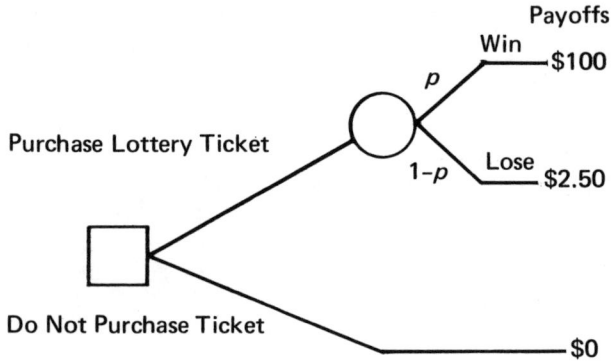

For example, suppose that the probability of winning is 0.01, that is, one chance in 100. The probability of losing is then $1 - 0.01$, or 0.99. The expected payoff associated with the decision to purchase a lottery ticket is

Expected payoff = $100(0.01) - \$2.50(0.99) = -\$1.48$

Now the branches emanating from the circle in Figure 5-2 may be pruned, or deleted, from the decision tree and replaced by the expected payoff, - $1.48. The pruned, or reduced, tree is shown in Figure 5-3.

Figure 5-3. Reduced decision tree for the lottery example.

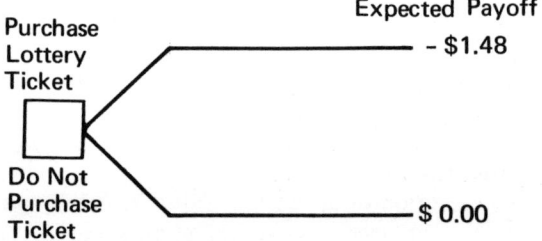

According to the criterion of selecting the action that minimizes expected payoff, it is clear that we would choose *not* to purchase the lottery ticket, since $0.00 is greater than - $1.48.

The basic procedure of replacing the branches that emanate from a chance *node,* or circle, is common to all decision tree analyses that use expected payoff criteria.

An additional concept, called the *rollback technique,* is added when the problem involves a sequence of interrelated decisions over time. The analysis is begun at the chronologically last decisions in the tree and rolled back to the immediate decision point. The rollback technique will be illustrated subsequently.

There is one final point before we move on to an illustration of the use of decision trees in investment analysis. Note that the chance events that follow a given action are *mutually exclusive* and *exhaustive.* In other words, the events cannot occur together, but one of the events *must* occur.

The Use of Decision Trees in Investment Analysis

The NCS Corporation has developed a new product that it wants to produce and market. The product is expected to have a life of approximately nine years. NCS does not currently have the facilities to manufacture the new product, however, and it must decide whether to build a plant for the purpose or subcontract for the manufacture. As we shall see, the management of NCS can use decision trees to advantage in evaluating the available choices.

Capacity for a new plant would be limited to that sufficient to meet forecast average demand. The limitation arises from NCS's current debt position and capital commitments; they constrain the initial investment to $2 million—the cost of a medium capacity plant. However, NCS expects its long-term position to improve in a few years, which will help it build a large plant or expand a smaller one at a future time. In fact, since NCS's experts estimate that about three years of production and marketing will elapse before they "get a good handle" on demand, the option to build or expand later provides some desirable flexibility.

In any case, near-term production is imperative if NCS is to secure a strong market position and maintain its leadership position in the field. As stated earlier, an alternative to the construction of a new plant is to secure the manufacturing services of an outside organization. That option is attractive because required initial outlays are small. Also, the contract route is less risky than the new-plant one. NCS management recognizes the value of contracting for about three years' production, or until demand can be more accurately forecast. At that time, the firm would still be free to exercise its option to build a medium- or large-capacity plant if demand were high enough to warrant the action.

Thus, in this situation, NCS has two immediate courses of action open: build a medium-capacity plant or contract for initial production. The choice is between the high-fixed-cost, low-variable-cost plant option and the low-fixed-cost, high-variable-cost contract option. Several future choices bear directly upon the immediate decision. They are given in Table 5-1.

Table 5-1. Relevant future decisions for NCS corporation.

Immediate Choices	Relevant Future Choices
1. Build medium-capacity plant	A. Expand plant B. Do not expand plant
2. Contract for initial 3-year production run	A. Build large plant B. Build medium plant C. Terminate project

Selection of Criteria

At the risk of repetition, one of the first steps in any investment analysis should be definition of objectives and selection of criteria to measure the degree to which each possible action attains the objectives. For brevity, let us assume that NPW is a meaningful measure of the "worth" of NCS's alternatives. The criterion that we shall apply is as follows: Select the course of action that yields maximum *expected* NPW. (Some comments on expected monetary value criteria are included at the end of this chapter and in Chapter 6.) The cost of capital for NCS, to be used in NPW calculations, is 15 percent.

Collection of Data for the NCS Decision Tree

The salient features of a decision tree are the acts, events, and payoffs. The present and future acts for NCS have already been outlined. The payoffs are net present values computed from the initial outlays and net cash flows resulting from the possible acts. Levels of demand are the chance events in this problem, and thus probability estimates must be provided for each demand level.

Although demand is actually a continuous variable, we have made the simplifying assumption that it has three discrete values: high, medium and low. (A brief discussion of the method of handling continuous events in decision trees has been included at the end of this chapter.)

Estimates of the initial outlays required by the several options are shown in Table 5-2. The initial investment for a large plant is approximately twice that for the medium-size one. The cost of building a medium-size plant today and expanding to large-plant capacity later exceeds the initial outlay for a large plant. The contract option requires a small initial outlay.

Table 5-3 shows estimates of expected annual cash flows that result from possible act-event combinations. For example, annual cash proceeds of $350,000 are expected if a medium-capacity plant is built and demand is low.

Table 5-2. Initial outlays for various actions.

Action	Initial Outlay at Time of Decision ($MM)
Build medium-size plant immediately	1.8
Build medium-size plant 3 years from now	2.0
Build large plant 3 years from now	3.5
Expand medium-size plant 3 years from now	2.2
Contract for outside manufacturing	0.1

Table 5-3. Annual net cash flow projections.

Manufacturing Method	Demand Level	Annual Net Cash Flow ($MM)
Large plant	High	2.0
Large plant	Medium	0.5
Large plant	Low	0.2
Medium-size plant	High or medium	0.8
Medium-size plant	Low	0.35
Contract	High or medium	0.5
Contract	Low	-0.1

Chance events (demand levels) are described by the data in Table 5-4. The data are probability estimates that must be provided as *input* in two ways. The first set of estimates applies to long-term or "average" demand. In addition, we have divided the market lifetime into two phases: the initial 3-year period and the final 6-year period. Thus, it is necessary to supply probability estimates for "compound events." Table 5-4 shows, for instance, that there is a 0.10 probability that demand will be high initially and medium in the long term.

The compound event probabilities reveal that long-term demand will never exceed initial demand and may in fact be lower. Thus NCS experts believe that competitive factors will play a major role in the long term.

Tables 5-5 and 5-6 show probability estimates that were derived from the input values. The estimates will be required for the decision tree.

The NCS Decision Tree

One version of the decision tree for NCS is shown in Figure 5-4. There are other versions, of course, but they

Table 5-4. Subjective probability estimates of demand.

Event	Probability That Event Will Occur
High long-term demand	0.15
Medium long-term demand	0.50
Low long-term demand	0.35

Compound Event		
Initial Demand	Long-Term Demand	Probability That Compound Event Will Occur
High	High	0.15
High	Medium	0.00
High	Low	0.00
Medium	High	0.10
Medium	Medium	0.40
Medium	Low	0.00
Low	High	0.03
Low	Medium	0.07
Low	Low	0.25

Table 5-5. Computed initial demand probabilities.

Event	Probability That Event Will Occur
High initial demand	0.28 = 0.15 + 0.10 + 0.03
Medium initial demand	0.47 = 0.40 + 0.07
Low initial demand	0.25

Table 5-6. Conditional probabilities.

Event A (Initial Demand)	Event B (Long-Term Demand)	Probability That B Will Occur Given That A Has Occurred
High	High	0.54 = 0.15/0.28
Medium	High	0 = 0/0.47
Low	High	0 = 0/0.25
High	Medium	0.36 = 0.10/0.28
Medium	Medium	0.85 = 0.40/0.47
Low	Medium	0 = 0/0.25
High	Low	0.10 = 0.03/0.28
Medium	Low	0.15 = 0.07/0.47
Low	Low	1.0 = 0.25/0.25

differ from the one presented primarily in the level of detail. Bear in mind that the purpose of the tree is to assist NCS management in choosing between the actions shown emanating from decision point 1 in the tree. (Note that decision points are indicated by squares and chance events by circles.) According to the criterion selected, we must ultimately determine the expected NPW for each of the possible actions.

Figure 5-4. Decision tree.

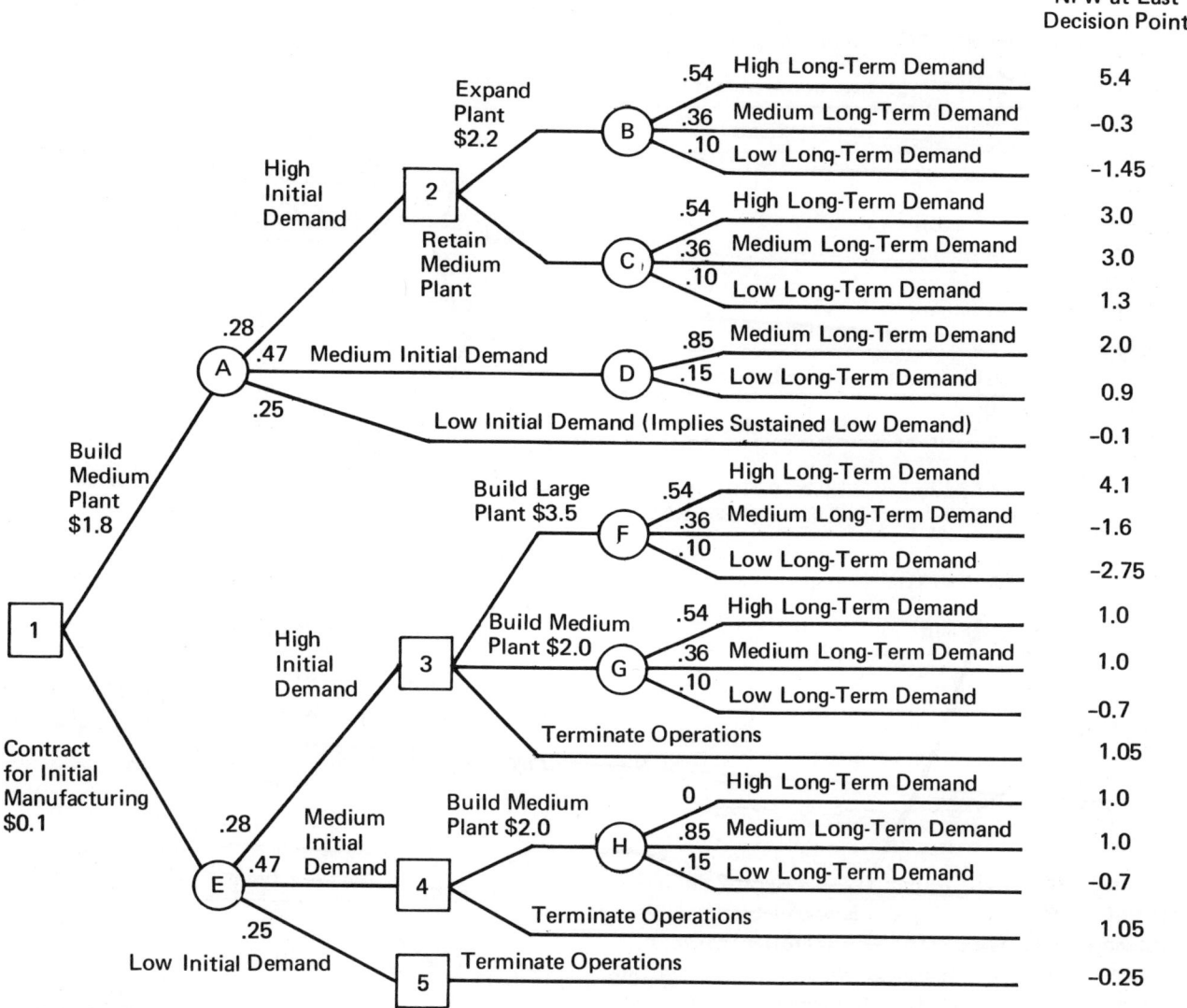

The Rollback Technique

The expected NPW of each immediate course of action is calculated by starting at the chronologically last of the decisions shown in the tree. Suppose that we are standing at decision point 2 (a medium-capacity plant has been constructed and initial demand for the product is high). What action should we take? Expand the existing medium-capacity plant in response to initially high demand or retain the existing plant as is?

The answer is straightforward because we have an objective criterion: maximizing expected NPW. Figure 5-5 provides the calculation of expected NPW for each action emanating from decision point 2. Note that expected NPW is $2.67 million for the expand-plant choice, as opposed to $2.83 million for retaining the medium-capacity plant as is. Thus, in the event that decision point 2 is reached, we would act optimally and maintain the medium-capacity plant for an expected NPW of $2.83 million. Now all the branches of the tree stemming from decision point 2 can be eliminated or pruned; the value $2.83 million replaces them. The same procedure would be applied at decision points 3, 4, and 5 and would result in the reduced tree shown in Figure 5-6.

All that remains is to compute the expected NPW as shown in Figure 5-6, and the result is the final decision tree, Figure 5-7. The option to contract for manufacturing is preferable to the new-plant action, because the

45

Figure 5-5. Determining the optimal act at decision point 2.

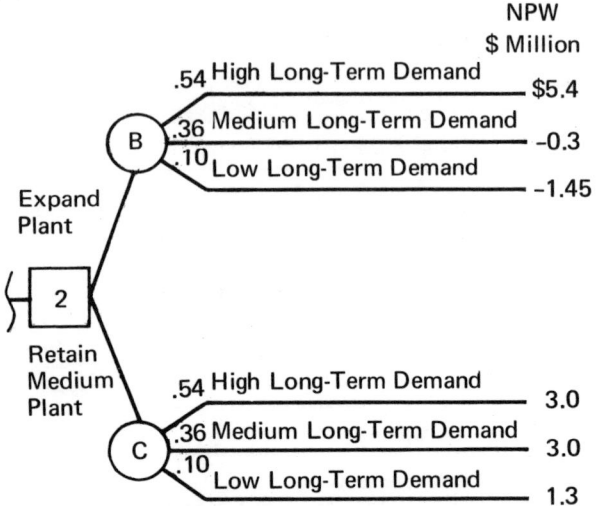

Expected NPW at B = 0.54(5.4) + 0.36(−0.3) + 0.10(−1.45) = $2.67
Expected NPW at C = 0.54(3.0) + 0.36(3.0) + 0.10(1.3) = 2.83

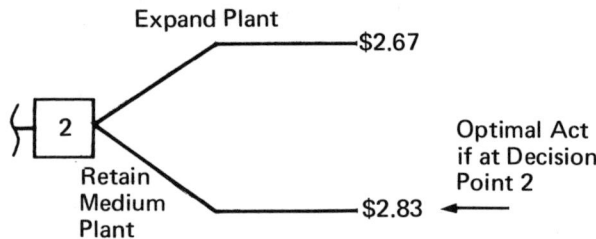

expected NPW of the former exceeds that of the latter. Moreover, the contract option is acceptable in an absolute sense, since its expected NPW is greater than zero.

Overall, the computation process consists in starting at the last decision points in the tree and rolling backward until the expected payoff for the immediate choices is determined. One additional point should be clarified here. In calculating the expected payoff at, say, decision point 2 in the NCS tree, we determine the present value *at the time that decision 2 is made.* Table 5-7 illustrates this point.

The Expected Value of Perfect Information

Firms often expend large amounts of money on efforts to improve the accuracy of demand forecasts. Decision trees can be used to determine an upper bound on the amounts that should be devoted to that kind of effort. The procedure is as follows. We compute the maximum expected payoff for the investment under the assumption that *perfect* information regarding the chance

Figure 5-6. A further reduced version of the decision tree.

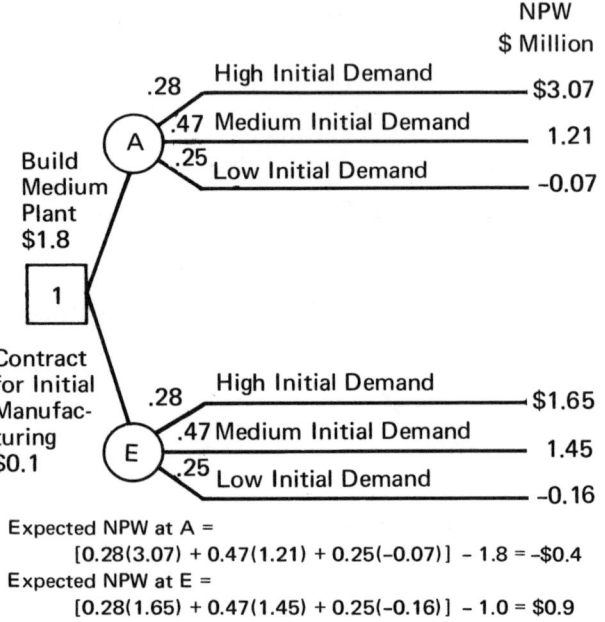

Expected NPW at A =
 [0.28(3.07) + 0.47(1.21) + 0.25(−0.07)] − 1.8 = −$0.4
Expected NPW at E =
 [0.28(1.65) + 0.47(1.45) + 0.25(−0.16)] − 1.0 = $0.9

Figure 5-7. The fully reduced decision tree.

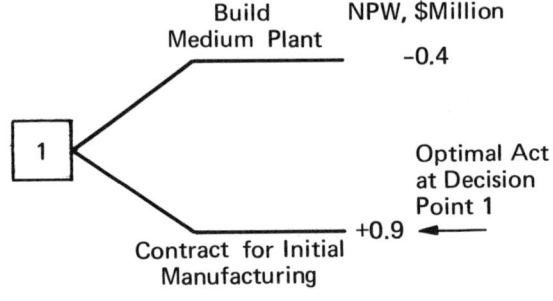

events is available. For example, if NCS knew in advance that initial and average demand would be high, it would opt for initial contract manufacture and subsequent construction of a large plant, since that sequence of acts maximizes payoff when initial and average demand are high. Table 5-8 shows the optimal courses of action for all possible demand sequences, assuming perfect knowledge. Note that the expected NPW would be $1.32 million if perfect information on demand levels were available. Since the expected NPW in the preceding case was

Table 5-7. Sample computation of an expected payoff at decision 2 in the NCS tree.

Illustrative Case

Assume that the medium-capacity plant is retained and long-term demand is low.

Initial Outlay

The initial outlay required to retain the medium-capacity plant is zero, since the $1.8 million initial outlay for the medium-capacity plant has already been spent and is thus a *sunk cost*.

Cash Flows

Years from Decision 2	Net Annual Cash Flow ($MM)	Present Value of $1 at 15%	Present Value of Cash Flow ($MM)
1	0.35	0.87	0.305
2	0.35	0.756	0.265
3	0.35	0.658	0.230
4	0.35	0.572	0.200
5	0.35	0.497	0.175
6	0.35	0.432	0.152

Present value ≅ 1.3

Table 5-8. The expected value of perfect information.

Initial Demand	Long-Term Demand	Probability	Optimal Sequence of Actions	NPW ($MM)
High	High	0.15	Contract for 3 years and then build large plant	3.35
High	Medium	0.10	Medium plant initially, no expansion	1.36
High	Low	0.03	Contract for 3 years and terminate at the end of that time	1.35
Medium	Medium	0.40	Contract for 3 years and terminate at the end of that time	1.35
Medium	Low	0.07	Contract for 3 years and terminate at the end of that time	1.35
Low	Low	0.25	Reject the entire project	0.00

Expected value of perfect information = [0.15(3.35) + 0.10(1.36) + 0.03(1.35) + 0.40(1.35) + 0.07(1.35) + 0.25(0)] − 0.9
= 1.32 − 0.90 = $0.42 million

$0.9 million, the expected present worth of perfect information is $0.42 million (1.32 − 0.9), or $420,000. Thus, it would not be rational to spend more than $420,000 to reduce demand uncertainty further.

Continuous Events in Decision Trees (Stochastic Decision Tree Analysis)

The NCS decision tree was simplified by assuming that demand would be at one of three discrete levels, but such a simplification is not essential. Figure 5-8 is an overview of the NCS decision tree based on the assumption of continuous demand levels. The outputs of that kind of decision tree are probability distributions of payoff rather than expected payoffs.

Since probability distributions display all the information that is available, a decision tree based on that kind of data is inherently superior to one based on expected value. The distributions corresponding to the node can be determined by simulation procedures. A discussion of the technique is presented in Hespos and Strassman. (2)

Figure 5-8. The decision tree assuming that demand is a continuous random variable.

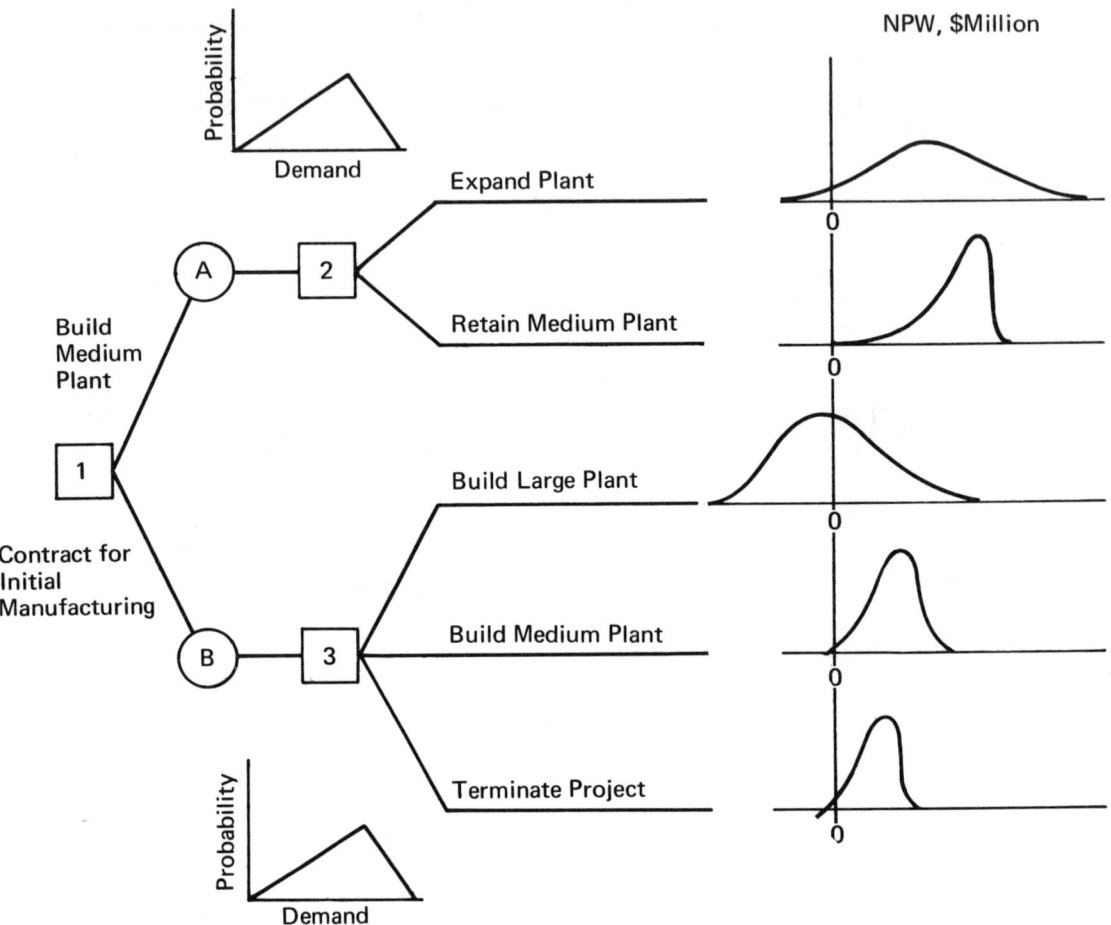

Expected Value and One-Time Events

Sometimes the use of expected payoff as a measure of worth of one-time events does not make sense. As Schlaifer points out, few of us would be indifferent to the choice between a certain $1 billion dollars and a 50-50 chance at $2 billion or nothing. Yet the *expected* monetary gains are equal for the two choices, which implies indifference if expected monetary value is used as a measure of worth. When expected monetary worth is not meaningful, some measures of *utility* are required. That concept is discussed in Chapter 6.

Summary

Decision trees are a systematic means of organizing and displaying all of the future *events* and *actions* that directly affect the consequences of present actions.

Before a decision tree can be utilized effectively, a criterion or set of criteria must be selected. Moreover, data must be collected and organized properly.

Optimal decisions are identified by applying the rollback technique.

It is not at all simple to understand the simple.

Eric Hoffer
The Passionate State of Mind

6
Intellectual Post-Processing

The title of this chapter, intellectual post-processing (IP^2), is a phrase coined by Norman Agin of MATHEMATICA to describe the set of activities that the analyst should undertake after he completes his preliminary evaluation of alternatives and before he presents results and makes recommendations to management. The objective of the activity is to gain insight into the decision problem by *questioning the assumptions* that underlie an analysis, *evaluating the consequences of alternative assumptions,* and, particularly, *seeking and evaluating new strategic alternatives.* In other words, the effort is to insure that the analysis of existing options is sound and that all reasonable options have been explored.

The post-processing activity is not only essential from the point of view of increasing the likelihood of a "correct" decision but also useful in contributing to the confidence of both the analyst and the decision maker in the results. That confidence is necessary if the analysis is to be of use in decision making. To be sure, that is equally true of any analysis, but it assumes special importance in a quantitative risk analysis because (at this point in time) many executives are unfamiliar with the tools and techniques employed. The unfamiliarity is often a basis for skepticism and a reluctance to accept the analyst's recommendations. Frustration with that attitude often engenders a response from the analyst known as the disinherited Messiah complex, which is, to say the least, no aid to effective communication. But communication is essential if the analyst is to do an effective job of objective analysis. If decision makers need to learn something from the analyst, so also does the analyst need to learn something from the decision maker. The analyst is by no means omniscient with regard to all the factors that enter into a decision, and he is as capable as anyone else of oversight. The following example cited by Brown (3) illustrates that very well:

> A corporate staff team at General Mills evaluated an acquisition opportunity by means of a DTA [decision tree analysis] computer program that took four months to develop and another two months to run with successively modified inputs corresponding to new assessments and assumptions made by the researchers and executives. In all, 140 computer runs were made before arriving at a recommendation to make the acquisition and to adopt a specific marketing and production strategy. The recommendation was rejected by top management, however, when the company's legal counsel advised against the acquisition on certain legal grounds. The lawyers discovered that a critical consideration had been omitted from the analysis which rendered it unusable for the purpose at hand.

Fortunately, in this case, everyone viewed it as a lesson learned, and subsequent applications at General Mills have been successful. (3) In another environment, the failure would have been the death knell of all theoretical (translation: unrealistic) approaches.

Granted, then, that IP^2 is an important activity, how can we undertake it in a systematic way? At the risk of oversimplification, there are perhaps seven key elements in IP^2. These are shown in the box below.

Key Elements in Intellectual Post-Processing (IP^2)

1. Relevance
2. Simplicity versus inclusiveness
3. Plausibility
4. Sensitivity analyses
5. Synthesizing alternatives
6. Contingency analyses
7. Qualitative factors

Have You Forgotten Any of These?

With the exception of item 7, we will discuss each of these elements in turn. You will observe as you read through the next few pages that most of the concepts are simple and straightforward. What is not so simple, however, is the implementation of the concepts. Therein lies the art of a good analysis.

Relevance

It is axiomatic that the analysis be relevant to the *decision at hand.* It is also true that, in the conduct of any analysis, many of the interesting and useful ideas that are developed might be worth exploring but are not relevant to the decision at hand. If the analysis is to be effective, consideration of those issues must be deferred. Many otherwise excellent analyses are unsatisfactory because they don't answer any question at all or because they answer the wrong question. Brown (3) furnishes an example of that failing:

> A central staff team for an international manufacturer of industrial components carried out a sophisticated and competent DTA designed to help a regional subsidiary choose which of several alternative markets to compete in. When the DTA part of the study was presented to the subsidiary's president, however, he perceived it as having little relevance to him in his decision making. He told me that the market forecast and other input data gathered for the analysis were certainly of substantial value to him, but he could not see that the DTA itself added much that was useful. Indeed, while the market data provided a basis for much of the subsidiary's subsequent strategy, no specific action appeared to be traceable to the DTA part of the study (though some people in the company felt that the analysis had some diffuse influence on several decisions).

In citing reasons for the lack of perceived utility, Brown continues:

> The decision options addressed by the DTA turned out *not* to be the ones the president was concerned about. (For example, he was more interested in deciding *how* to develop a particular market sector than in *whether* to be in it at all.) Fuller and earlier communication between executive and staff analysts helps to counter this very common problem experienced in applying DTA.

As Brown suggests, better communication between the analyst and the executive is helpful, but is not a total solution. There may be controversy within the boardroom itself on what exactly the decision at hand is; moreover, the answer to that question is highly dependent upon what the perceived options are. A good analysis should suggest additional options. Communication between the analyst and the executive furnishes what *must be included* (otherwise, the analysis is not responsive), but some creative thought often pays dividends. Perhaps the most useful advice to the analyst is to continually ask himself, "How does the work I am doing contribute to solution of the real problem?"

Simplicity Versus Inclusiveness

The fundamental trade-off in any analytical study is simplicity versus inclusiveness. The aim of a balanced analysis is to keep the analysis as simple as possible, that is, to include only the factors that are important to the outcome of the decision. That applies to both the models employed and the alternatives that are finally recommended for executive action.

There is good reason to keep the models simple. First of all, complex models can fool the analyst as well as the decision maker. Furthermore, complex models often have a large number of assumptions that are easy to forget once the models are constructed. Finally, complex models require more data that, aside from being tedious to obtain, are frequently at a level of detail that effectively prohibits careful attention to data validity. A simple model is not the same thing as a naive model; it is naive only with respect to problem aspects that are unimportant to the decision at hand.

There is also good reason for simplicity (economy) with respect to the alternatives that are finally recommended to management for decision. That is not intended to limit *evaluation* of alternatives; rather, it is to limit the number of alternatives that are recommended for decision. What we are saying is that dominated alternatives should be eliminated. One alternative is said to be dominated by another if it is inferior in every respect to the other. For example, with respect to *quantitative* measures of project worth, an alternative investment A might dominate an alternative B if it is superior with respect to *expected* return and *variability* of return.

Two approaches are useful in detecting dominance; they are called *a fortiori* and *breakeven analysis.* A fortiori analysis refers to a technique whereby we make highly favorable assumptions with respect to numerical estimates for alternative A and highly unfavorable estimates for alternative B. If under those extreme conditions B still looks better than A, then A is said to be dominated by B. In breakeven analysis on the other hand, we seek to determine conditions under which both alternatives have the same return, or uncertainty of return, and then ask whether those conditions are probable. If they are judged to be highly improbable, then dominance exists.

As simple as the two approaches to detecting dominance seem to be, they are often effective in reducing the number of alternatives to be presented to management or, failing that, in making a strong case for the favored alternative. Testimony to their utility can be found in Kahn and Mann (12):

> *More than any other single thing, the skilled use of a fortiori and breakeven analyses separate the professionals from the amateurs.* Most analyses should (conceptually) be done in two stages: a first stage to find out what one wants to recommend and a second stage that generates the kind of information that makes the recommendations convincing even to a hostile and disbelieving, but intelligent audience.

Plausibility

Another useful way to screen an analysis is to evaluate the plausibility of results. Are the results consistent with intuition? That implausible results are obtained from an analysis does not necessarily imply that they are incorrect, but it does suggest the wisdom of further examination. Implausible results are most often due to implicit assumptions that are incorrect, or to errors in computer programming or the input data. Sometimes, however, the results are entirely correct and intuition is wrong. In a real sense, that is a highly desirable state of affairs because it vividly demonstrates the utility of analytical techniques.

How can we best evaluate the "plausibility" of the results? The most obvious way is to inspect the output histograms of measures of investment worth and ask such questions as the following two: Is it reasonable that alternative A has a higher expected return than alternative B under the given set of assumptions? As we change some of the assumptions, is it reasonable that differences between the alternatives should narrow?

If the results are contraintuitive, it is necessary to dig deeper to try to find the reason why the analysis does not square with expectation. Perhaps models are being used for situations in which the assumptions do not hold; perhaps the data need to be reexamined; or perhaps our intuition is at fault. Whatever the cause, it is necessary to track it down and make appropriate modifications to our models, data, or intuition. Sensitivity analysis reports (which will be discussed in the next section) sometimes provide useful clues as to where to look.

Another useful device is to examine a series of individual simulation trials or typical iterations. A good computer program for risk analysis should have an option to provide that information. We have found it best to have the information organized in a format that is conventionally employed within the company (perhaps the format used in capital expenditure request forms). Table 6-1 shows a typical simulation trial for the large-plant alternative discussed in the example given in Chapter 1. By an examination of such a typical iteration (particularly one with extreme returns) unusual conditions can be detected and the analyst and executive can gain a feel for the characteristics of the investment. Also, the report helps executives understand and visualize the simulation technique.

Sensitivity Analysis

One of the reasons for getting misleading results from a risk analysis is the use of incorrect inputs. The analyst should play devil's advocate with respect to the input estimates throughout the analysis effort. However carefully he does so, errors in estimation will persist.

Fortunately, the investment outcome is not uniformly sensitive to errors in the input factors. Herein enters *sensitivity analysis,* which amounts to learning which variables are most important to the outcome of a given investment. Sensitivity analysis has been widely used in many quantitative areas, but only recently has it come into use in investment analysis and risk analysis. In fact, as recently as 1968 it was the subject of a doctoral dissertation in business administration. (11) Some useful reference material in this area are papers by Rappaport and Drews (16), Thorne (20), and Maeffi. (13)

Table 6-1. Typical simulation trial.

Alternative 1: large plant.	Contingency: scenario 1 (surprise-free).					
	Year					
	1	2	3	4	5	6
Total revenue	997	2,612	3,450	3,753	3,601	3,454
Price	0.85	0.82	0.78	0.75	0	0.69
Sales	1,173	3,203	4,410	5,000	5,000	5,000
Prime variable costs						
Raw materials	312	851	1,170	1,325	1,323	1,321
Processing	98	268	368	417	417	417
Transfer variable costs						
Distribution	68	185	254	287	286	286
Other variable costs						
Total variable costs	478	1,303	1,791	2,020	2,026	2,624
Contribution before fixed costs	519	1,300	1,659	1,724	1,574	1,431
Fixed costs						
Fixed cost one	285	294	302	311	320	329
Fixed cost two	83	86	88	91	94	97
Total fixed costs	368	370	390	402	414	426
Book depreciation	115	115	115	115	115	115
Net operating profit	36	815	1,153	1,207	1,045	889
Cumulative of above	36	851	2,005	3,212	4,257	5,147
Before-tax income (NC investment)	151	930	1,268	1,322	1,100	1,004
Cumulative of above	151	1,931	2,359	3,872	4,832	5,837
Total investment	2,300	0	0	0	0	0
Residual value of investment						1,150
Net cash flow (no discount)	187	555	711	732	648	1,718
Cumulative of above (with investment)	−2,113	−1,559	−848	−116	532	2,250
Net cash flow (discount = 0.10)	170	458	534	500	402	970
Cumulative of above (with investment)	−2,130	−1,672	−1,138	−638	−230	734
Net cash flow (discount = 0.16)	161	412	456	404	309	705
Cumulative of above (with investment)	−2,139	−1,727	−1,271	−867	−559	146

The return on investment for this trial was 17.875%.

In its simplest form, a sensitivity analysis can be conducted by replacing the input variables by their expected values and then determining nominal values for all measures of investment worth. Following the initial determinations, the input factors are perturbed a like amount (or percentage) and the change in the calculated measures of worth is noted. For example, the following equation relates pretax profit P to sales level s, sales price p, variable cost c, and period fixed costs FC.

$$P = s(p - c) - FC$$

Now suppose that expected values for the variables are s = 800 units, p = $0.80 per unit, c = $0.55 per unit, and FC = 100. Substitution of those values into the equation results in a profit P of $100. If the sales volume were to increase 5 percent to 840 units, the profit would increase to $110, or by 10 percent. By making similar computations for each of the factors in the equation, we arrive at the results shown in Table 6-2. Note that *equal percentage* changes imply that profit is most sensitive to changes in price p, followed by changes in variable cost, sales volume, and fixed cost in that order.

Table 6-2. Sensitivity analysis (equal percentage changes) of the equation $P = s(p-c)$ - FC.

A 5% increase in this variable	would increase the variable to	and result in profits of	for a percentage change of	Rank order (Out of 4)
Sales (units)	840	$110	10%	3
Price ($/unit)	0.84	$132	32%	1
Variable cost ($/unit)	0.5775	$78	−22%	2
Fixed cost ($)	105	$95	−5%	4

Our sensitivity analysis has been useful in apprising us of the *consequences* of a stated percentage change, but not necessarily of the *likelihood* of the change. Although a 5 percent increase in price may have a greater effect on profit than a 5 percent increase in variable cost, it may be much less—or more—likely. The way to take that possibility into account is to make *equally likely* changes as opposed to equal percentage changes. To see how to do so, examine Figure 6-1, which shows a CDF for the level of sales. A 5 percentile increase from the mean (which is equal to the median of a symmetrical distribution function) would increase the sales level from 800 to 815 units, which would increase profits to 103.75, or by 3.75 percent (note the difference between a 5 percent increase and a 5 percentile increase).

The results of similar computations for the other variables are shown in Table 6-3. Note how consideration of the likelihood of error changes our conclusion with respect to the relative importance of price and variable cost. We believe that the method of perturbations is to be preferred to that on which Table 6-2 is based.

In practice, of course, the models are considerably more complex than the equation $P = s(p-c) - FC$, and the output from a sensitivity analysis is more likely to appear as shown in Table 6-4. The actual model employed for the analysis required some 50 variables. Inspection of Table 6-4 indicates that terminal share of market and initial selling price are the most important variables (rank order 1 and 2, respectively). It has been our experience and that of others (see Refs. 11, 13, 16, 20) that price and sales volume are often highly important factors (at least in areas of low or mature technology).

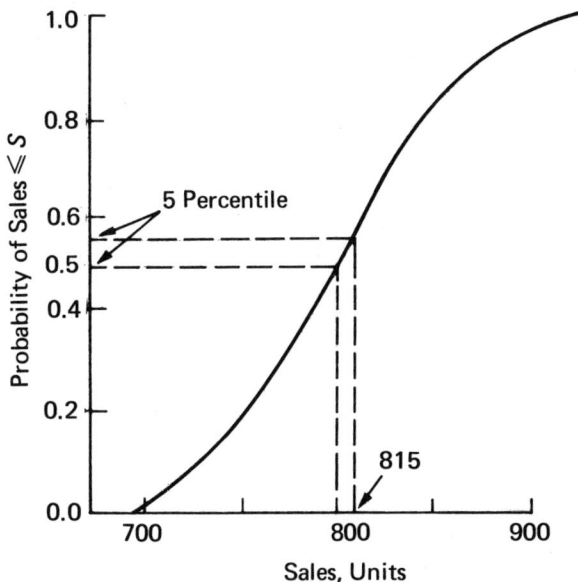

Figure 6-1. Determination of magnitude of percentile change in probability distribution of sales.

Table 6-3. Sensitivity analysis (equal percentile changes) of the equation $P = s(p-c) - FC$.

A 5 percentile increase in in this variable	would increase the variable to	and result in profits of	for a percentage change of	Rank order (Out of 4)
Sales (units)	815	103.75	3.75%	3
Price ($/unit)	0.81	108	8%	1
Variable cost ($/unit)	0.56	92	-8%	1
Fixed cost ($)	101	99	-1%	4

Table 6-4. Illustrative sensitivity analysis for net present worth (10 percentile one-at-a-time change).

Input Variable	Expected Value of Input Variable	Value with 10 Percentile		Change in NPW as Percent of Average Value		Rank Order* in 50 Variables
		Incr.	Decr.	Incr.	Decr.	
Terminal share of market (%)	15	16	14.5	12%	-14%	1
Total market size in year 1 (millions)	8.0	8.5	7.5	5%	-5%	7
Total market growth rate (%/year)	6	6.3	5.8	7%	-5%	4
Initial selling price ($/unit)	0.75	0.78	0.71	8%	-9%	2
Variable manufacturing cost ($/unit)	0.120	0.125	0.115	-4%	4%	10
Working capital factor	0.23	0.25	0.21	-1%	1%	21

*Based upon average absolute change.

Another way to gain insight into the sensitivity of the measures of investment worth to input factors is to inspect what is termed, in military risk analysis, an impact matrix. A matrix coefficient is the percentile increase or decrease in one factor necessary to exactly offset a stated percentile increase in any other factor. Table 6-5 shows part of an impact matrix. By referring to that table, we can see that a 10 percentile increase in factor 1 would be exactly offset by a 21 percentile decrease in factor 2 and also that there is no possible increase in factor 6 that would offset a 10 percentile increase in factor 1, 2, or 3.

Table 6-5. Illustrative impact matrix for net present worth.

A 10 percentile increase in this factor	would be offset by the percentile increases in these factors					
	1	2	3	4	5	6
1		−21	−16	−15	+31	NP*
2	−17		−10	− 7	+13	NP
3	−14	− 7		− 9	+18	NP
4						
5						

*NP means that there is no possible increase in this variable sufficient to offset the perturbation of the indicated variable.

As useful as sensitivity analyses are, it is wrong to regard them as a panacea. They have limitations. The first is that it is possible to determine the sensitivity of investment only with respect to the factors represented in the model. Though self-evident, that is a point often overlooked. Second, gross errors in guesstimation of levels of variables can distort the sensitivity assessments. Figure 6-2 shows how the NPW of an investment might vary with the economic life of that investment. From 3 to 6 years, the NPW is strongly dependent upon economic life, whereas from 6 years onward, that sensitivity declines markedly. If the actual economic life were 4 years, for example and it was incorrectly estimated to be 8 years, not only would the estimate be in error but the economic life would not appear to be an important variable.

A third problem with sensitivity analysis is that usually correlations between factors are neglected—sometimes because they are unknown. In the original example, sales and price were implicitly assumed to be independent variables, whereas they probably are not. In fact, an increase in price may bring about a decrease in sales. In the event that a demand relationship can be estimated, the assumption of independence need not be made. However, for many products, demand relationships are unknown, and they are, moreover, difficult to measure. In spite of those shortcomings (and one or two others not mentioned) sensitivity analysis, when it is carefully conducted, is one of the most useful IP^2 activities.

Figure 6-2. The sensitivity of a variable may be a function of the level of that variable.

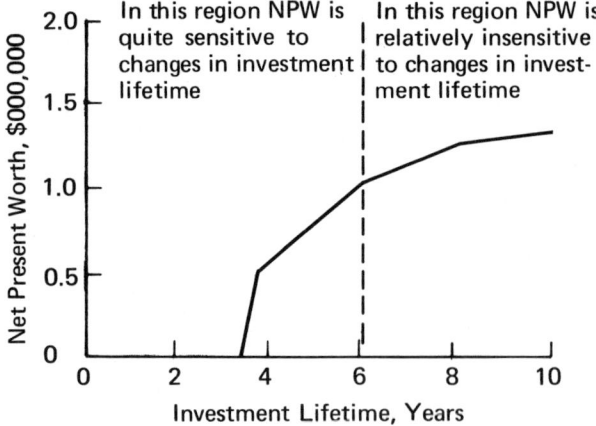

Synthesis of Alternatives

Joel Dean (4), writing in *Harvard Business Review*, put failure to consider investment alternatives at the top of a list of fallacies of capital expenditure evaluation when he stated some years ago:

> Perhaps the most common mistake in analyzing a capital proposal is the failure to consider any alternatives. There are always alternatives to an investment proposal, and a systematic analysis of the alternatives is the benchmark for estimating both the investment and the earnings of a capital project. What will happen if the requested investment is not made measures what the company will get out of it if the investment is made.

Throughout his career at Ford, and later as Secretary of Defense, Robert McNamara insisted that his subordinates define and evaluate sufficient alternatives, whether for a proposed plant expansion (Why not absorb necessary production at other plants? Why not build another plant with more efficient technology?) or a proposed missile system for the Army, Navy, or Air Force (Can existing missiles from other services be modified? Are defensive systems more efficient than offensive ones? Is the expansion of conventional forces more cost effective?). Example after example can be cited to indicate that a major problem of decision making in general, and in respect to capital investments in particular, is the failure to consider sufficient alternatives.

It is our view that one of the major benefits of a quantitative investment analysis can be the genesis of alternatives. That is true because it is easy to exercise analytical or computer models once developed and also because the process of generating inputs as outlined in Chapter 4 often suggests alternatives.

Contingency Analysis

Numerical estimates that are inputs to an analysis are always made with respect to a set of assumptions. If we consider a different set of assumptions, it is likely that several of the input distributions will be altered. In some cases, we are relatively confident of those assumptions; in others, there are alternative sets of assumptions only somewhat less likely than those used initially. By a contingency analysis, we mean one or a series of exercises of the model designed to evaluate the consequences of the alternative assumptions (often termed *scenarios* in military planning).

As an example of what we mean, consider the chemical plant investment problem discussed in Chapter 1. You may recall that estimates of sales were made on the assumption of a relatively stable marketplace (that is, of a supply-demand relationship in the future similar to that of the past). Suppose, however, you had reason to believe that another chemical company was actively considering entry into the market or expansion of existing capacity. If the capacity addition were large enough, it might have a marked impact on demand and price estimates. (For example, in the chemical industry some years ago, several firms simultaneously entered the polypropylene market, which resulted in a substantial imbalance of demand and supply and caused prices to tumble.)

Suppose a sensitivity analysis indicated that price and volume are significant factors. It would then be important to assess the impact of that intelligence. To do so, we would obtain revised inputs for demand and price on the assumption of competitive entry. Similarly, we would repeat the process for other sets of assumptions that are plausible and relevant. Figure 6-3 illustrates the way in which the results of such an analysis might be organized and presented to management. The exhibit shows histograms of NPW for various investment alternatives under various contingencies. The main conclusions to be drawn from inspection of the histograms are as follows:

1. Under anticipated market conditions (the surprise-free scenario) the large-plant alternative offers not only a higher expected return but also both a higher variability of that return (and a higher probability of loss) than the graduated-entry alternative.

Figure 6-3. Study results. Histograms are shown for net present worth.

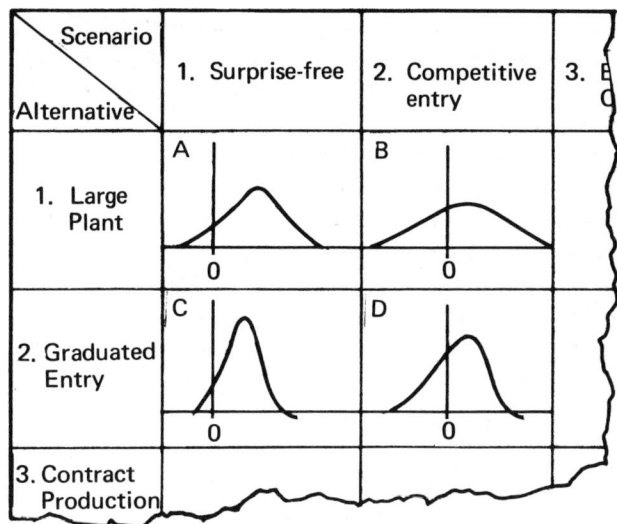

WHICH ALTERNATIVE WOULD YOU SELECT?

2. The principal effect of competitive entry into the market is to lower the expected return of both investment alternatives. However, the expected return of the large-plant alternative is decreased more than that of the small-plant alternative to the extent that both alternatives offer approximately the same expected return (compare B with D in Figure 6-3). The variability of return for the graduated-entry alternative is still substantially less than that for the large-plant alternative.

3. A secondary effect of competitive entry is to increase somewhat the variability of return of each investment alternative. That is so because demand estimates become more uncertain in the event of competitive entry.

The risk-adverse executive, faced with this decision, might well choose the graduated-entry alternative. The chain of reasoning that underlies the choice might be as follows: Under the assumption of competitive entry both alternatives offer the same expected return, but graduated entry offers less variability. Thus in those circumstances, I would clearly prefer D to B. Even in the surprise-free case, the higher expected return offered by the large-plant alternative is not worth the additional risk of loss.

Utility Assessment

In our discussion of the outputs of a risk analysis, we illustrated distribution functions of measures of investment worth and implied that the decision maker can make judgments on the utility of an investment by inspecting such distributions in an implicit and intuitive manner. In general, however, it has been our experience

55

that the determination of the distributions for alternative investment strategies and scenarios is a practical limit to the formal analysis. Similar sentiments are expressed by Hillier (9, 10) and Borch. (2) Nonetheless, there are alternatives for further analysis that attempt to develop systematic procedures for reducing distributions to a single measure of the *utility* of a given investment opportunity. We will discuss one such approach—the one that is, in our judgment, most practical—in this section. Some useful references that advocate and illustrate the techniques are books by Schlaifer (17), Raiffa (15), and Bierman and Smidt (1), and articles by Swalm (19) and Hammond. (8)

The approach is best illustrated by example rather than discussion. The basic conceptual device behind the approach is that of the standard reference gamble or standard lottery proposed by Morgenstern and Von Neumann. (21) To illustrate how it operates, suppose that you are offered a lottery ticket that has a 0.50 probability of winning a prize of $10,000 and a 0.50 probability of winning nothing. What price would you be willing to pay for it? One notion of a fair purchase price is the expected value of the winnings, which is $5,000; and a person willing to pay $5,000 is said to be *risk indifferent*. Most businessmen would offer something less than the expected value. The specific amount might well depend upon such factors as current asset position and whether the prospective purchaser felt lucky. The point, though, is that there exists a price at or beneath which the lottery is an attractive proposition. That price is termed by Raiffa the *certainty monetary equivalent* (CME) of the lottery. Suppose, upon reflection, that you decided that $2,500 was your CME. Clearly, a lottery with a zero probability of winning the $10,000 would be worth $0 to you (if it would be worth more than that, please contact us immediately, because we have an abundant supply of such opportunities), whereas a lottery with a unit probability of winning (that is, certainty) would be worth $10,000.

Figure 6-4 is a graph that depicts the relationship between the lottery probability and the monetary equivalent. In fact, there is a functional relationship, termed a *utility function,* between those variables. To help show that function, let's ask you what a lottery ticket with a 0.75 probability of winning is worth. Suppose $5,000 is the answer. That answer helps to determine another point on your preference or utility curve, which is drawn through the points on Figure 6-4.

We can get some insight into your proclivity for risk taking by observing where your preference curve falls. A person who is indifferent to risk will have a curve that is a straight line connecting the two points (0,0) and ($10,000, 1.0). Curves that lie above the risk indifference line are characteristic of risk-adverse behavior; curves that fall beneath the line are characteristic of risk-prone behavior.

Figure 6-4. Relationship between lottery probability and monetary equivalent.

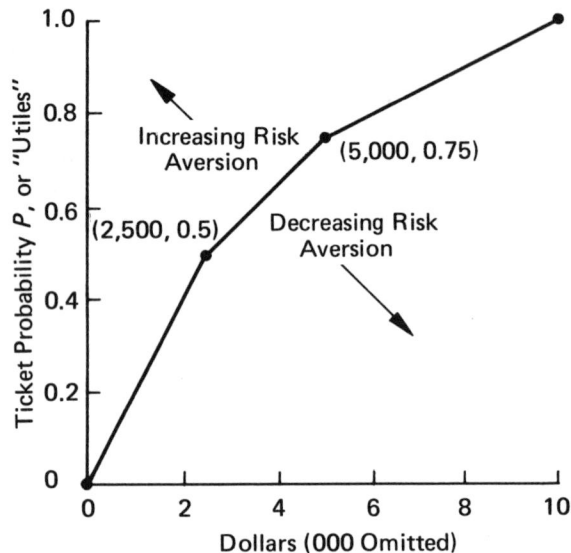

The important feature of the lottery is that it provides a useful, although somewhat artificial, way to get you to disclose your preference or utility curve for money. We could just as well label the ordinate in Figure 6-4 "utiles," or something equally convenient, as label it probability. How can we use the curve just obtained to help us evaluate the utility of investments having risk? The procedure is quite simple. Suppose we had an investment with just two NPW outcomes, say $2,000 and $8,000, and that the respective probabilities of the outcomes were 0.4 and 0.6. By referring to our curve in Figure 6-4 we find that the utility corresponding to an outcome of $8,000 is 0.82, whereas that corresponding to $2,000 is 0.42. The expected utility is 0.4(0.42) + 0.6(0.82) or 0.66, which, from our curve corresponds to a CME of $3,800. An extremely well reasoned and intuitively appealing argument for the legitimacy of that procedure can be found in Raiffa. (15) Note that the expected return of the investment is 0.4(2,000) + 0.6(8,000) or $5,600, which is significantly in excess of the subjective worth of the investment.

The extension to multiple outcomes is straightforward. Figure 6-5 shows the risk analysis output distribution of NPW for a hypothetical venture. Shown beneath is a utility curve for the decision maker. That is all the information necessary for us to determine the CME for the investment. To illustrate, there is a 0.05 probability of obtaining an NPW of 375,000 (the midpoint of the interval 350,000 to 400,000). That corresponds to a utility of 0.96 on the decision maker's preference curve (follow the dashed line). Similarly, there is a 0.05 probability of obtaining an NPW of 325,000 or 0.92 utiles, and so on. The expected utility of the investment is calculated to be about 0.65, which corresponds to a CME of $110,000. As in the preceding example, the CME is less than the expected NPW of the investment ($130,000).

Figure 6-5. Illustration of process of obtaining certainty monetary equivalent from risk analysis output distribution.

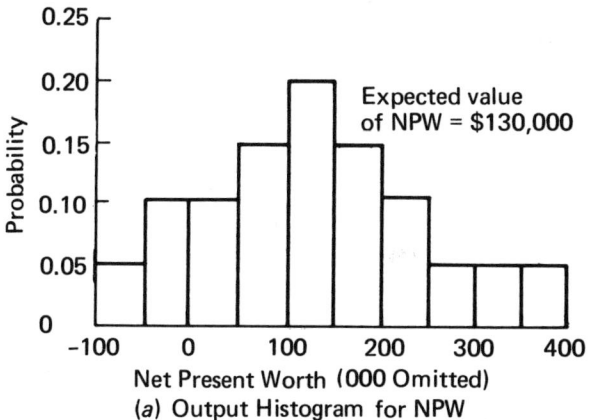

(a) Output Histogram for NPW

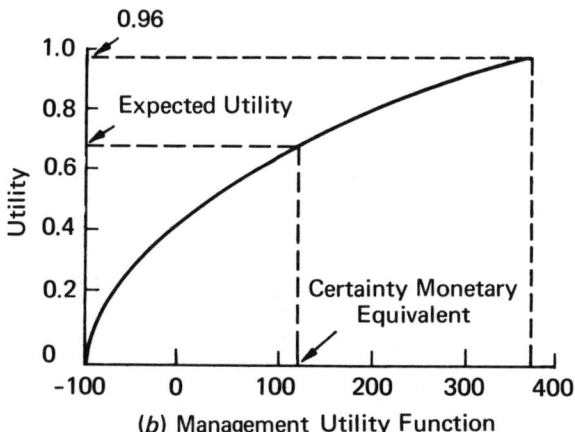

(b) Management Utility Function

Expected utility
= 0.05(.96) + 0.05(.92) + 0.05(.90) + 0.10(.84) + 0.15(.75)
+ 0.20(.68) + 0.15(.56) + 0.10(46) + 0.10(.35) + 0.5(.19) = 0.65

Certainty monetary equivalent
[from graph (b)] = $110,000

Let's explore the consequences of the preceding discussion and examples. The implication is that, if it is possible to determine the decision maker's utility function, then it is possible to condense the entire distribution of investment outcomes to one meaningful number that reflects *all* the monetary consequences of a given investment alternative. The procedure is analogous to the discounting procedures used in NPW calculations. Just as those procedures discount for the futurity of cash flows and thus correctly reflect the time value of money, so this procedure discounts for the uncertainty of cash flows and thus correctly reflects the decision maker's attitude toward risk.

The usefulness of the approach hinges upon two related issues. First, is it possible to elicit preference functions of the type discussed? Second, are businessmen likely to understand and "feel comfortable" with the analyses? The answer to the first question is a qualified yes; that to the second is in our view at present unresolved.

Regarding the first issue, there have been a number of reportedly successful attempts to determine preference or utility functions. In particular, the works of Swalm (19), Mosteller and Nogee (14), Grayson (6), and Green (7) are worth reading to gain some idea of the state of the art. Those studies have had some interesting results. Figure 6-6 shows some typical utility curves that have been constructed for businessmen. The studies of Swalm reveal that preference profiles often appear as shown by curve 1 of the figure. The noteworthy characteristic of that curve is the precipitous drop in utility for monetary equivalents near zero. The "zero illusion," as christened by Hammond (8), is a persistent feature of utility functions and probably reflects the asymmetrical reward function for the businessman as an *individual* within the corporate framework.

Figure 6-6. Some typical utility curves for businessmen.

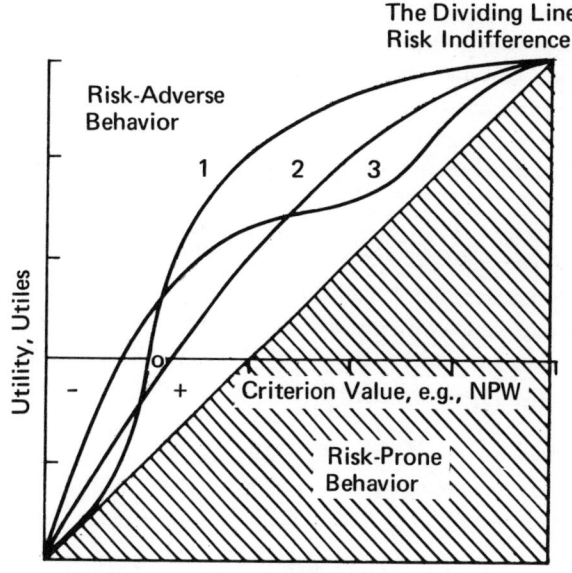

1. Swalm survey respondent
2. "Rational" risk averters
3. Grayson oil wildcatters

Curve 3 is representative of certain businessmen, notably oil wildcatters interviewed by Grayson. (6) The humps in the curve represent threshold amounts for levels of achievement or levels of aspiration, according to Siegel. (18) Increasing rewards above a given level increases utility to the decision maker only slightly until another plateau (for example, joining the Fortune 500 or becoming a millionaire) is reached. Curve 2 is that of a "rational" or "model" risk averter. Hammond argues that many executives who might initially opt for curve 1 switch to curve 2 upon reflection.

From the studies referred to, it appears that, under controlled conditions, it is possible to elicit consistent preference information, but whether the information elicited is credible to the decision maker is much more uncertain. It will take time for the new concepts to diffuse throughout the management community. That, of course, was true of risk analysis. Only a few years ago, in 1956, the editors of *Fortune* (5) remarked with accuracy:

> Freud said that it takes a high degree of sophistication to believe in chance. By this measure most executives are sophisticated, since they acknowledge the role of chance in the "fate" of their decisions. They are not, however, sophisticated enough to use chance consciously as an instrument of decision.

Today, risk analysis is fairly well known and accepted in the business community. Thus we are optimistic about the use of utility theory by tomorrow's businessmen.

References

Chapter 1

1. R. M. Adelson, "Criteria for Capital Investment: An Approach Through Decision Theory," *Operational Research Quarterly*, March 1965, pp. 19-50.

2. "The Use of Simulation in Analyzing Investment Decisions," notes for AMA course for division and plant controllers, New York, August 11-15, 1969.

3. R. G. Brown, *Smoothing, Forecasting and Prediction of Discrete Time Series* (Englewood Cliffs, N.J.: Prentice-Hall, Inc., 1963), p. 444.

4. R. V. Brown, "Do Managers Find Decision Theory Useful?" *Harvard Business Review*, May-June 1970, pp. 53-64.

5. R. A. Byrne, A. Charnes, W. W. Cooper, and K. Kortanek, "Some New Approaches to Risk," *The Accounting Review*, Vol. 63, No. 1, pp. 18-37.

6. P. F. Dienemann, "Estimating Cost Uncertainty Using Monte Carlo Techniques," The Rand Corporation, RM-4854-PR, Santa Monica, Calif., 1966.

7. A. M. Economos, "A Financial Simulation for Risk Analysis of a Proposed Subsidiary," *Management Science*, Vol. 15, No. 12, pp. 675-682.

8. B. M. George, "The Weapon Systems Development Process," in *Government Procurement and Contracting*, Part 9, Hearings Before a Subcommittee of the Committee on Government Operations, House of Representatives, Ninety-first Congress, First Session on H.R. 474 (1969), pp. 2491-2520.

9. H. M. Hawkins and O. E. Martin, "How to Evaluate Projects," *Chemical Engineering Progress*, December 1964, pp. 58-63.

10. D. B. Hertz, "Investment Policies That Pay Off," *Harvard Business Review*, January-February 1968, pp. 94-106.

11. ——, "Risk Analysis in Capital Investment," *Harvard Business Review*, January-February 1964, pp. 143-154.

12. R. F. Hespos and P. A. Strassmann, "Stochastic Decision Trees for the Analysis of Investment Decisions," *Management Science*, Vol. 11, No. 10, pp. 244-260.

13. S. W. Hess and H. A. Quigley, "Analysis of Risk in Investments Using Monte Carlo Techniques," *Chemical Engineering Progress Symposium Series 42*, Vol. 59, pp. 55-63.

14. F. Kafka, *Parables and Paradoxes* (New York: Schocken Books Inc., 1961), p. 93.

15. J. C. T. Mao, *Quantitative Analysis of Financial Decisions* (Toronto: Collier-Macmillan, Canada, Ltd., 1969), pp. 553ff.

16. P. Massé, *Optimal Investment Decisions: Rules for Action and Criteria for Choice* (Englewood Cliffs, N.J.: Prentice-Hall, Inc., 1962), pp. 198-248.

17. J. H. Norton, "The Role of Subjective Probability in Evaluating New Product Ventures," *Chemical Engineering Progress Symposium Series 42*, Vol. 59, pp. 49-55.

18. C. Pacifico, "Is It Worth the Risk?" *Chemical Engineering Progress*, Vol. 60, No. 4, pp. 19-21.

19. E. L. Reynard, "Risk Analysis in Chemical Plant Investment," *Industrial and Engineering Chemistry*, July 1966, pp. 61-64.

20. M. B. Solomon, "Uncertainty and Its Effect on Capital Investment Analysis," *Management Science*, April 1966, pp. 334-339.

21. *Survey of Current Business*, Vol. 51, No. 4, pp. 11ff.

22. J. R. Virts and R. W. Garrett, "Weighing Risk in Capacity Expansion," *Harvard Business Review*, May-June 1970, pp. 84-93.

23. D. H. Woods, "Improving Estimates That Involve Uncertainty," *Harvard Business Review*, July-August 1966, p. 136.

Chapter 2

1. H. B. Bierman and S. Smidt, *The Capital Budgeting Decision: Economic Analysis and Financing of Investment Projects* (New York: The Macmillan Company, 1966).
2. J. L. Bower, *Managing the Resource Allocation Process: A Study of Corporate Planning and Investment* (Boston: Division of Research, Graduate School of Business Administration, Harvard University, 1970).
3. V. H. Brown, "Rate of Return: Some Comments on Its Applicability in Capital Budgeting," *The Accounting Review,* January 1961, pp. 50–62.
4. G. A. Christy, *Capital Budgeting: Current Practices and Their Efficiency* (Eugene, Oreg.: Bureau of Business and Economic Research, University of Oregon, 1966).
5. E. Dale, *Management: Theory and Practice* (New York: McGraw-Hill Book Company, 1969).
6. J. Dean, *Capital Budgeting* (New York: Columbia University Press, 1951).
7. ———, "Measuring the Productivity of Capital," *Harvard Business Review,* January–February 1954, pp. 120–130.
8. H. E. Dougall, "Payback as an Aid in Capital Budgeting," *The Controller,* February 1961, pp. 86–88.
9. G. Fisher, *Cost Considerations in Systems Analysis* (New York: American Elsevier Publishing Company, Inc., 1970).
10. J. W. Gardner, *Self-Renewal: The Individual and Innovative Society* (New York: Harper & Row, Publishers, Incorporated, 1964).
11. W. W. Haynes, *Managerial Economics: Analyses and Cases* (Austin, Tex.: Business Publications Inc., 1969).
12. C. J. Hitch and R. A. McKean, *The Economics of Defense in the Nuclear Age* (New York: American Atheneum, 1965).
13. E. M. Lerner and A. Rappaport, "Limit DCF in Capital Budgeting," *Harvard Business Review,* September–October 1968, pp. 133–139.
14. R. J. Reul, "Profitability Index for Investments," *Harvard Business Review,* July–August 1957, pp. 116–132.
15. M. F. Usry, *Capital-Expenditure Planning and Control* (Austin: Bureau of Business Research, The University of Texas, 1966).
16. M. Weingartner, "Some New Views on the Payback Period in Capital Budgeting," *Management Science,* August 1969, pp. B594–B607.

Chapter 3

1. A. C. Enthoven and K. W. Smith, *How Much Is Enough? Shaping the Defense Program, 1961–1969* (New York: Harper & Row, Publishers, Incorporated, 1971), p. 322.
2. T. Fabian, "Operations Research in Corporate Financial Management," MATHEMATICA report.
3. M. G. Kendall, "Introduction to Model Building and Its Problems," Chap. 1 in CEIR Ltd., *Mathematical Model Building in Economics and Industry* (London: Charles Griffin & Company, Ltd., 1966), p. 3.
4. J. H. Lorie and L. J. Savage, "Three Problems in Rationing Capital," *Journal of Business,* October 1955, pp. 229–239.
5. J. C. T. Mao, *Quantitative Analysis of Financial Decisions* (Toronto: Collier-Macmillan, Canada, Ltd., 1969).
6. H. Markowitz, *Portfolio Selection: Efficient Diversification of Investments* (New York: McGraw-Hill Book Company, 1959).
7. R. D. Specht, "The Nature of Models," Chap. 10 in E. S. Quade and W. J. Boucher (Eds.), *Systems Analysis and Policy Planning: Applications in Defense* (New York: American Elsevier Publishing Company, Inc., 1968), p. 212.
8. L. Savage, *The Foundations of Statistics* (New York: John Wiley & Sons, Inc., 1954).

Chapter 4

1. S. E. Asch, "Effects of Group Pressure Upon the Modification and Distortion of Judgments," Eleanor E. Maccoby et al. (Eds.), *Readings in Social Psychology,* 3d Ed. (London: Holt, Rinehart and Winston, Inc., 1958).
2. G. E. P. Box and G. M. Jenkins, *Time Series Analysis, Forecasting and Controls* (San Francisco: Holden-Day, Inc., Publisher, 1970).
3. R. G. Brown, *Smoothing, Forecasting and Prediction of Discrete Time Series* (Englewood Cliffs, N.J.: Prentice-Hall, Inc., 1963).
4. R. Campbell, "A Methodological Study of the Utilization of Experts in Business Forecasting," Ph.D. dissertation, University of California at Los Angeles, 1966.
5. J. C. Chambers, S. K. Mullick, and D. D. Smith, "How to Choose the Right Forecasting Technique," *Harvard Business Review,* July–August 1971, pp. 45–74.
6. N. C. Dalkey, "The Delphi Method: An Experimental Study in Group Opinion," The Rand Corporation, RM-5888-PR, Santa Monica, Calif., 1969, p. 50.

7. ——, "Experiments in Group Prediction," The Rand Corporation, P-3820, Santa Monica, Calif., 1968.

8. ——, "Delphi," The Rand Corporation, P-3704, Santa Monica, Calif., 1967.

9. N. C. Dalkey and O. Helmer, "An Experimental Application of the Delphi Method to the Use of Experts," *Management Science,* Vol. 9, No. 9.

10. N. C. Dalkey, "Experiments in Group Prediction," The Rand Corporation, P-3820, Santa Monica, Calif., 1968.

11. N. C. Dalkey, B. Brown, and S. Cochran, "Use of Self-rating to Improve Group Estimates," *Technological Forecasting,* Vol. 1, No. 3, pp. 283-291.

12. G. Hadley, *Introduction to Business Statistics* (San Francisco: Holden-Day, Inc., Publisher, 1968).

13. O. Helmer, "Systematic Use of Expert Opinions," The Rand Corporation, P-3721, Santa Monica, Calif., 1967.

14. ——, "Convergence of Expert Consensus Through Feedback," The Rand Corporation, P-2973, Santa Monica, Calif., 1964.

15. ——, "The Systematic Use of Expert Judgment in Operations Research," The Rand Corporation, P-2795, Santa Monica, Calif., 1963.

16. D. B. Hertz, "Risk Analysis in Capital Investment," *Harvard Business Review,* January-February 1964, p. 148.

17. J. Johnston, *Econometric Methods* (New York: McGraw-Hill Book Company, 1960).

18. H. H. Kelly and J. W. Thibaut, "Experimental Studies of Group Problem Solving and Process," in Gardner Lindzey (Ed.), *Handbook of Social Psychology,* Vol. II (Reading, Mass.: Addison-Wesley Publishing Company, Inc., 1954).

19. R. F. Maier, "Assets and Liabilities in Group Problem Solving: The Need for an Integrative Function," *Psychological Review,* July 1967, pp. 239-249.

20. W. T. Morris, *The Analysis of Management Decisions* (Homewood, Ill.: Richard D. Irwin, Inc., 1964), pp. 8-10, 49-50.

21. J. B. Quinn, "Technological Forecasting," *Harvard Business Review,* March-April 1967, p. 38.

22. H. Raiffa, *Decision Analysis, Introductory Lectures on Choice Under Uncertainty* (Reading, Mass.: Addison-Wesley Publishing Company, Inc., 1968), pp. 162-167.

23. R. Schlaifer, *Analysis of Decisions Under Uncertainty* (New York: McGraw-Hill Book Company, 1969), pp. 214-215.

24. R. L. Winkler, "The Consensus of Subjective Probability Distributions," *Management Science,* Vol. 15, No. 2, pp. 61-76.

25. D. H. Woods, "Improving Estimates That Involve Uncertainty," *Harvard Business Review,* July-August 1966, pp. 91-98.

Chapter 5

1. J. S. Hammond, "Better Decisions with Preference Theory," *Harvard Business Review,* November-December 1967, pp. 117ff.

2. R. F. Hespos and P. A. Strassman, "Stochastic Decision Trees for the Analysis of Investment Decisions," *Management Science,* Vol. 11, No. 10, pp. 244-260.

3. J. F. Magee, "Decision Trees for Decision Making," *Harvard Business Review,* July-August 1964, pp. 126ff.

4. ——, "How to Use Decision Trees in Capital Investment," *Harvard Business Review,* September-October 1964, pp. 79ff.

5. R. Schlaifer, *Analysis of Decisions Under Uncertainty* (New York: McGraw-Hill Book Company, 1969).

Chapter 6

1. H. B. Bierman and S. Smidt, *The Capital Budgeting Decision: Economic Analysis and Financing of Investment Projects* (New York: The Macmillan Company, 1966).

2. K. H. Borch, *The Economics of Uncertainty* (Princeton, N.J.: Princeton University Press, 1968), p. 17.

3. R. V. Brown, "Do Managers Find Decision Theory Useful?" *Harvard Business Review,* May-June 1970, pp. 60, 62.

4. Joel Dean, "Measuring the Productivity of Capital," *Harvard Business Review,* January-February 1954, p. 26.

5. The Editors of *Fortune, The Executive Life* (Garden City, N.Y.: Doubleday & Company, Inc., 1956), p. 175.

6. C. J. Grayson, *Decisions Under Uncertainty* (Boston: Harvard Business School, 1960).

7. P. E. Green, "Risk Attitudes and Chemical Investment Decisions," *Chemical Engineering Progress,* January 1963, p. 35.

8. J. S. Hammond, "Better Decisions with Preference Theory," *Harvard Business Review,* November-December 1967, pp. 117ff.

9. F. S. Hillier, "Derivation of Probabilistic Information for the Evaluation of Risky Investments," *Management Science,* April 1963, pp. 443ff.

10. ——, *The Evaluation of Risky Interrelated Investments* (London: North-Holland Publishing Company, 1969), p. 29.

11. W. C. House, Jr., *Sensitivity Analysis in Making Capital Investment Decisions,* Research Monograph 3, National Association of Accountants, New York, 1968.
12. H. Kahn and I. Mann, "Techniques of Systems Analysis," The Rand Corporation, RM-1829, Santa Monica, Calif., 1956.
13. R. B. Maeffi, "Simulation, Sensitivity and Management Decision Rules," *Journal of Business,* Vol. 31, No. 3, pp. 177-186.
14. F. Mosteller and P. Nogee, "An Empirical Measurement of Utility," *Journal of Political Economy,* October 1951, pp. 371ff.
15. H. Raiffa, *Decision Analysis: Introductory Lectures on Choice Under Uncertainty* (Reading, Mass.: Addison-Wesley Publishing Company, Inc., 1968), pp. 57-60.
16. L. A. Rappaport and W. P. Drews, "A Mathematical Approach to Long-Range Planning," *Harvard Business Review,* May-June 1962, pp. 75-87.
17. R. Schlaifer, *Analysis of Decisions Under Uncertainty* (New York: McGraw-Hill Book Company, 1969).
18. S. Siegel, "Level of Aspiration and Decision Making," *Psychological Review,* Vol. 64, No. 2, pp. 253ff.
19. R. O. Swalm, "Utility Theory: Insights into Risk Taking," *Harvard Business Review,* November-December 1966, pp. 121ff.
20. H. C. Thorne et al., "How to Evaluate Chemical Projects," *Petroleum Refiner,* Vol. 40, No. 3.
21. J. von Neumann and O. Morgenstern, *Theory of Games and Economic Behavior* (Princeton, N.J.: Princeton University Press, 1944).

72
74
75
76
77
81
83
89